DISCOVER *Yourself*

in the

Women of the BIBLE

Tina~
May God
continue this good
work in you and
may this study
bless you as you
bless others!

Love,
Michele Giletto

Lessons from the Leading Ladies
of the Old Testament

MICHELE GILETTO

DEDICATION

This study is dedicated to the women I've met along the way, particularly the women with whom I've encountered the Living Water. You are the real women who display to the world the holy yet ordinary characteristics of the Bible's leading ladies.

In a special way, this study is dedicated to my children Basil John and Martha. God graciously blessed us when He made us a family. Everything I do and every word I write is ultimately to bless you as I serve Him. I love you both to the moon and back. Immeasurable love fills my heart because I am your mom.

This teaching has been handed down from the One who loves us fully, wholly and forever. As I ran in the spring of 2013…He wrote.

His inspired Word fills these pages.

TABLE OF CONTENTS

Acknowledgements

There is another story in these pages and it is the story of a woman with a commission on her heart to produce this book amidst many competing priorities. Because of this, there is an army of people who have supported this effort over the past few years.

A huge thank you to Barb at Rooted Publishers who patiently worked with me in the publishing of this study. Thank you for helping me to finally reach this finished product.

To my Gathered in Grace sisters, you are amazing prayer warriors and I thank you from the bottom of my heart for showing me radical love for Jesus and for being willing to pray at any moment, day or night, for any reason. I love you.

My *She Leads* conference sisters who have dedicated their lives to speaking and equipping women to love Jesus and others well while working in the home, marketplace and ministry. In a special way, thank you to Verna, Linda, Lori, Lisa, Michelle, Tina, Veirdre, Kenya, Laura, Sarah, Lauren and Sue. Your inspiration and encouragement are fingerprints all over these pages. I love you each and thank God for the blessing you are.

To Jessie Seneca, *She Leads* founder and leader, for your unwavering belief and love for me since the first day we met in your Bible study. Every time we are together, I learn more about Jesus by the way you love and serve Him. You are a beautiful friend, mentor and gift to me and so many.

To the Women Gathered online community who teaches me more than I could ever teach them about the Word of God and how to live it out in our daily lives. Your trust and reliance on Christ is based on your knowing that His grace is sufficient in any circumstance and it is humbling to have a front row seat and bear witness as God increases in your life.

To Deborah Lovett for walking through many of life's fires with me since meeting in 2012. I thank God for you and the friendship He has blessed us with. Your prayers have held me up more than you will ever know and have given me the courage many times to keep on going.

To my sister by choice, Jane George, an amazing example of grace and leadership. You are a beautiful symbol of God's redeeming love and power. I was blessed in a

i

mighty way that fateful day we met.

Linda and Jeff Green for being on the front lines of my faith development over the past ten years. Thank you for opening my eyes to God's Word, living and active, and for the many faith filled conversations we have shared. Thank you for challenging me with tenderness and encouraging me in everything I do. I love you both and the family you created together more than words can express. We have the best family! This Old Testament is dedicated in a special way to you, Jeff, for igniting in me a love for the ancients.

To my sister and editor, Dr. Yvonne McCarthy for manning the front line of my life since the beginning. Thank you for slogging through these edits and for polishing my grammar and challenging me when necessary. Thank you for seeing the Holy Spirit's inspiration through these pages and through my life. You are more than a sister. More than a friend. We share a heart and a soul and I'm so grateful to you and love you so much. Thank you for sharing Joe with us and for the many ways you both love and serve so freely. Thank you for the gift of family and for sharing your beautiful family with mine!

To my parents Eugene and Yvonne Green. Dad, I miss you every day and thank God for choosing us to be the dynamic duo we always were. Mom, you are a beautiful example of God's love. The way you show your love for us through so many big and little ways. You are always there with the right thought at the right time. You are the smartest woman I know, and I thank God that He picked you for me. I love you so much!

To Basil Paul, you have been my greatest teacher. I can't imagine how my life would have been without you and all we have been through together. Thank you for always believing in me. I will always believe in you and love you.

To Basil John and Martha who made us a family. My heart is full every time I look at you. I have never loved anyone more than I love the two of you. You are the greatest cheerleaders and supporters a mom could ever have. God created us for each other. We have been through so much and learned so many hard things together, yet through it all God's grace and love were all around us. Thank you for seeing His hand in all of this and in our lives. You are the reason God created me. You are the reason that I do everything. I love you both so much!

To my sweet Jesus, I am undone each and every time I consider how great your love for me. Thank you for speaking into my life in so many powerful ways. Thank you for walking alongside me and for carrying me through the darkest days. Thank you for giving it all up for me that day on Calvary. I love you so much and now I live for you. To you be all glory, praise and honor!

Prologue

My life did not turn out at all the way I expected it to. Life is a funny thing. You think you are playing by one set of rules and then it's as though everyone got a memo that the rules changed, but you.

You grow up dreaming that life will be one way, and then it's as though that road is blocked and every other way through is a major detour. Is it just me, or has this happened to you?

Yet, some of those detours take us on incredible pathways that we may have missed if we had stayed on the first road. This Bible study is one of those incredible pathways born from a period of five years of deep prayer and conviction in the quiet moments of the morning: just me and God.

In 2008, my husband lost his job. That single event changed the trajectory of our lives. He fell into a deep depression that has lasted since and his health literally broke. A series of neurological issues and Parkinson like symptoms began to take over. I dealt with it the only way I knew how, I cried and I prayed.

My dream of being a stay-at-home mom and raising our adopted children was now dashed. I would be returning to work and deemed the provider for our family. A major detour.

I was visiting my sister-in-law and brother just after the realization of this had hit me. I had two small children, a sick husband, an elderly mother-in-law that we cared for and now I would be returning to full time work. I was beside myself. I don't recall what my sister-in-law Linda said to my brother first, but next she said, *"Jeffrey, what do you want her to do"*? Without missing a beat, my brother turned to me, pointed and said, *"You need to put your nose in the Word of God, and you need to keep it there"*.

I shook my head "Ok" and went out that day to buy a new Bible. (It didn't occur to me at the time that I probably had four or more Bibles at home...) From that day forward, my life changed. God placed an unquenchable desire in my spirit for His Word. I had not grown up learning the Bible. This was a whole new, big, incredible world that he unlocked for me.

His Word is the balm that soothes every ache and pain this world can give. His Word is the life and light that keeps the breath in my body and the hope of a new day alive in my heart. His Word is His gentle and loving reminder that I am deeply loved, called by name and preciously protected. His Word is true and reminds me that this current life is temporary, but life in Him is eternal.

His Word strengthened me and gave me the courage to step out in faith and take that detour, and I am so glad I did! Although the struggles and circumstances grew, no matter what we faced, we have been okay, because we know *"… the Bible is the infallible Word of God, inspired by the Holy Spirit, and contains every answer to our problems"*. (2 Timothy 3:16-17, 2 Peter 1:20-21)

The other life-sustaining and life-giving activity I did was run. To look at me, you would not know I have a deep love affair with strapping on my sneakers and taking to the road or the treadmill. In 2013, five years after I began my intense daily Bible study and prayer time, God began to reveal the study you hold in your hands to me on my daily runs. He placed names of Biblical heroines on my heart, prodding me to press in to figure out who these women were and what He desired I share about them.

Thank you for taking a slight detour on your journey to go on this special road trip with me through the Bible. I pray that as you meet Scripture's leading ladies, you will learn a little more about yourself and a lot more about the awesome, loving God we serve.

Introduction

Women

Women are important to the heart of Jesus. All women: every shape, size, profession, color and creed. Throughout Biblical history, women were chosen by God to accomplish His holy purpose, starting with the first woman who was created to give company to her man. These women can feel so far-off from us and yet when we take a close look at their lives, we can see ourselves. God uses both men and women to further His holy will.

I work with predominately all women in both my day job and in ministry and I know that many women do not feel this worth. So let me convince you of your important contribution, not only to God, but to the world. Did you know:

- Women are responsible for 80% of all healthcare decisions made in the United States?
- Women are more empathetic, better communicators, value and often achieve work-life balance?
- Women have a high emotional intelligence and handle crises better than their male counterparts?

God the Father, Son and Spirit all desire to have a personal relationship with their sons and daughters. You were chosen by God, since before the beginning of time, to be counted among His holy ones. You – a woman!

God desires us to seek Him, men and women alike, and the Bible is filled with references to this fact. Scripture repeatedly reminds us of God's promise that if *"we seek Him, we will find Him when we seek Him with all our heart."* (Jeremiah 29:13) He desires we *"call upon Him, come and pray to Him."* (Jeremiah 29:12) Yes, a close and personal relationship is what God desires for us. Jesus' life was an example of this. The Gospels record the many times that Jesus retreated to pray and seek His Father's voice. Heaven need not be separated from us any longer. We can be up close and personal with God by the same example of Jesus Christ.

Imagine that the God, whose breath drew creation from formless and empty space, would love you enough to send you His one and only Son. Deity sent to earth to walk and live among us. Can we just stop right there? The thought of it has me undone.

Jesus. Son of God. Born of a simple woman and raised by ordinary parents. This is amazing when you think about it. God could have sent His Son on a chariot through the clouds. He could have sent Him to the top of the mountain and commanded the winds and surf and all people to listen and obey. Yet God chose the same entrance into humanity for His Son that He has chosen for you and me. Birth to ordinary, hard-working people. Joseph and Mary. Humble. Lowly. It's inspiring to think that God allowed this humble woman to have so much influence over His Son.

We meet Jesus long before His birth in Bethlehem is announced by the Gospel writers. We see Jesus in the desert with Hagar, when she has given up and is without food or drink waiting to die. We see the foreshadowing to His birth in the miracle of the elder Sarah's birth of her long-awaited son Isaac. We meet woman after woman under great duress, whose life tells a story of transformation after having an encounter with the Holy God of Israel.

My life was transformed, too, when I met this man Jesus, and decided to work with great consistency and intentionality to have a personal relationship with Him. Like many of the women we will study, it took a big crisis in my life to put me on my knees in prayer and to grow a desire in my heart to dig into the Word of God so that I might know Him. What I didn't expect to happen though, was that as I was learning more about Him *I discovered more about me.*

And that is where this study begins. It begins with a realization that the people we hear about on Sunday are much more than saints in the greatest story of all time. They were real people. They felt the same things you feel, and they experienced the same struggles you experience. From Eve through all the women Jesus met along the way, we encounter story after story of these very holy, yet ordinary women.

My hope is that through this study, you will learn more about yourself and you will begin to see yourself as Christ sees you. From the resilience of Eve to the holiness of Esther, you will encounter women who are just like you. These heroines of Scripture may appear set apart, holy and far off from our daily experience, but through this study you will see *we are all the same!*

Yes, women matter to the heart of Jesus. *You* matter to the heart of Jesus. He loves you exactly how you are today, and I can hear Him calling you to draw closer to Him through His Word and through these stories that He handpicked to share with you right now.

Over the next five weeks, we are going to get real, up close and personal with these leading ladies of Scripture. By the end of this study, I suspect that you will begin to see more of yourself on the pages of the Bible – and that's what this book is all about: **For you to come to know the overwhelming, inspiring, never-failing, all-consuming, amazing love the Father has for you!**

This book can be experienced on its own, or you can share this book with a group and work through it as a Bible study. I have left some space within these pages for you to reflect, or you could answer the questions posed here in a special journal. To help you as you study, I have made every effort to break the week down into these five days of teaching~

Day 1 – We take a historical look at our leading lady

Day 2 – We discuss the major theme of her story

Day 3 - We reflect on her relationship with God

Day 4 – We consider her role as leader

Day 5 - We meditate on how God redeemed her

Unless specified otherwise, each Bible verse shared in this study is taken from the New International Version translation.

Now, open your Bible, get out your journal or index cards and let's get ready to get personal with Scripture's leading ladies!

. . . .

That is what this book is all about:

For you to come to know the overwhelming, inspiring, never-failing, all-consuming, amazing love the Father has for you!

Part I

Eve

1

Beginnings

"In the beginning" Genesis 1:1

We begin our study of female heroines at the beginning. Genesis. The book of beginnings. Let's open our Bibles and let the very first words of Scripture soak into our hearts:

> *[1] In the beginning God created the heavens and the earth. [2] Now the earth was formless and empty, darkness was over the surface of the deep, and the **Spirit of God was hovering over the waters.***

> *[3] And God said, "Let there be light," and there was light. [4] God saw that the light was good, and he separated the light from the darkness. [5] God called the light "day," and the darkness he called "night." And there was evening, and there was morning—the first day.*

Recently, while spending some time at the beach, I meditated on this sweet opening passage of Scripture. I had walked to the beach to watch the sunrise early one morning and there appeared over the body of water a haze of light so beautiful. I felt as though it was truly the Spirit of God, Himself, hovering over the water as Genesis 1 recalls. It was captivating and made this opening passage of Scripture very personal and very real. That experience brought heaven so close to me as though God, Himself, was bringing the very first words of Scripture alive. It was a glimpse of His holiness that I will never forget, and I allowed it to serve as a new beginning in my own spiritual quest for holiness.

The word genesis itself is defined as "the origin or formation of something." An origin. A beginning. So, we ask, what is Genesis the beginning of?

Creation. Humanity. God's mercy and blessing. The recorded Word of God. Your personal journey through the timeless lessons of Scripture to discover yourself. Unfortunately, it is also the beginning of sin and its effect. And death. Until that one glorious Sunday brought victory once and for all!

For now, let's begin at the beginning.

Please stop a moment and read the entire first chapter of Genesis. Try to picture what is being described on these pages. Imagine in your mind God's breath creating a hurling and shaking energy needed to create a sun in the sky and what it was like as His glory was illuminated for the first time! Imagine as He created each star to guide the night and the crescent moon that would grow into fullness each 30 days. Read and let your mind imagine as He breathed into creation the waters that would nourish this world for all time. Imagine. Read and be captivated as His love pours out those first five days.

"…and God saw that it was good." (Genesis 1:10)

After reading Genesis, a song of praise poured from my lips. It went something like this:

Father, thank You for Your love which is everlasting and unfailing. From the beginning of creation, You have provided in abundance for Your beloved. Thank You for every good blessing that You have given me, particularly the people You have entrusted to my care; the home that provides shelter and respite from the day; the food that fuels my body and the rest that restores my soul. I praise You and thank You!

What are you feeling after you read the story of creation, realizing that God saw as the highpoint of His masterpiece the creation of you and me? After reading the first chapter, write your song of praise to God for showing his love for you through creation in such a good way:

Go Deeper...
All this for me?

Humans were created on Day 6. Do you marvel at that? God spent the first five days preparing our banquet table. He created a beautiful universe that could sustain us and meet our every need as well as every want. Imagine God spent five out of his six days of creation working for our benefit and pleasure. This is a God who loves you! Before you were even created, God had provided for your every need and desire. God in his benevolence desired the best for every one of us. He entrusted to us dominion over his entire creation. And God blesses us and says to us,

> *"Be fruitful and increase in number; fill the earth and subdue it. Rule over the fish of the sea and the birds of the air and over every living creature that moves on the ground." Genesis 1:28*

Ponder for a moment this amazing gift and responsibility. Your father in

Heaven loved you enough to give you dominion over His creation. Dominion over His love poured out for you. Dominion over everything! Think of the people and things in your life that you have influence over. What kind of steward have you been to this blessing from God?

Father, thank You for the many blessings You so freely bestow upon us. Bless my friend as she works through this study and may she never forget the abundant love You have for her. Let today be a new beginning, a genesis, that brings her closer to You and all that You have created her to be. In Jesus' name, I pray. Amen.

2

Tempted

"Then the Lord God said, 'It is not good for the man to be alone, I will make a helper who is just right from him.' ...While the man slept, the Lord God took out one of the man's ribs and closed up the opening. Then the Lord God made a woman from the rib, and he brought her to the man."
Genesis 1:18, 22

"After women, flowers are the most lovely thing God has given the world."
Christian Dior

As a child, I often wondered if I had one less rib than my brother when I heard the above Scripture verse. I learned later, that we are anatomically all the same. God created woman from man, for man and formed her to be man's companion. We are his spiritual, emotional and physical partner.

On our good days, we cherish that role. We desire to be a good wife, a true help-mate, and that desire to please man is real. It is what our Father intended when He created us. However, as we were made in His image and likeness, we may also have our own ideas, dreams and hopes that differ from our male counter-part.

Eve certainly did. Here we are early in the book of Genesis and we are meeting a modern woman. A woman who we will quickly learn makes decisions. A woman who did not wait for permission to act when she saw what she wanted. She acted on her own thoughts and desires as so many of us do.

We face temptations every day. Sometimes they are big and easy to see like a direct advance made by a member of the opposite sex. Sometimes the temptations are less easy to spot like when friends are gossiping or prying. Sometimes the temptation comes from selfish desires: we want what we want when we want it.

That's what happened to Eve. She had the opportunity to display faithfulness and devotion to God, but instead she is won over by the forbidden fruits appeal. Her curiosity to know what she was missing was greater than her desire to keep what God had promised for her. Temptation wins. She could have waited. She could have trusted her Abba Daddy when He told her to stay away from the tree. Instead, she played into the hand of the enemy because *he was telling her what she wanted to hear.*

The result of giving into temptation? Sin. And from sin is born consequences.

Humanity would no longer enjoy God's rest and presence in the perfect Garden of Eden. Instead we begin writing a story wrought with fear, guilt and war. Alas, a different kind of beginning.

Let's look at what happened. Before we read Genesis chapter three, it's important to return to Genesis chapter two for just a moment. After God finished creating all things, this happens:

5 The Lord God took the man and put him in the Garden of Eden to work it and take care of it. 16 And the Lord God commanded the man, "You are free to eat from any tree in the garden; 17 but you must not eat from the tree of the knowledge of good and evil, for when you eat from it you will certainly die." Genesis 2:15-17

Okay, let's turn to Genesis chapter three. Here are a few verses from the New Living Translation Bible to get you started:

"The serpent was the shrewdest of all the wild animals the LORD God had made. One day he asked the woman, "Did God really say you must not eat the fruit from any of the trees in the garden?"

"Of course we may eat fruit from the trees in the garden," the woman replied. "It's only the fruit from the tree in the middle of the garden that we are not allowed to eat. God said, **'You must not eat it or even touch it; if you do, you will die.'** *"You won't die!" the serpent replied to the woman. "God knows that your eyes will be opened as soon as you eat it, and you will be like God, knowing both good and evil." (Emphasis added.)*

The woman was convinced. She saw that the tree was beautiful, and its fruit looked delicious, and she wanted the wisdom it would give her. So she took some of the fruit and ate it. Then she gave some to her husband, who was with her, and he ate it, too. At that moment their eyes were opened, and they suddenly felt shame at their nakedness. So they sewed fig leaves together to cover themselves.

When the cool evening breezes were blowing, the man and his wife heard the LORD God walking about in the garden. So they hid from the LORD God among the trees. Then the LORD God called to the man, "Where are you?" He replied, "I heard you walking in the garden, so I hid. I was afraid because I was naked." "Who told you that you were naked?" the LORD God asked. "Have you eaten from the tree whose fruit I commanded you not to eat?" The man replied, "It was the woman you gave me who gave me the fruit, and I ate it." (Genesis 3:1-12) NLT[1]

Did you see what happened here?

- Satan waited patiently as the woman grew in her confidence – a God confidence that had been born and nurtured by His love.
- Satan then tempts the woman and influences her by telling her something she longs to hear.
- The woman incorrectly re-states what she believed God said to her. He said, "Don't eat." She heard, "Don't eat or even touch." This made it even more tempting. She increased the temptation by her own thought.
- The woman is disobedient to God and obedient to her selfish desires.

- There are consequences for the woman's actions and the effect is wide-reaching.

Scripture tells us that the serpent was crafty. He poked his way into Eve's life and gained enough trust to push his agenda forward and she complied. Eve learned a major lesson that fateful day in the garden. So did Adam. He certainly has some responsibility in all of this. His role was to lead Eve, not simply stand by and then point fingers. The reality is our sins affect more people than just us. We don't always want to believe that. Ask the addict who claims, "the only person I'm hurting is myself." No. Anyone who you are in contact with will be affected. In the same way grace pours off us unto others, so does the consequence of sin. Sin affects more people than simply the sinner.

The other lesson, that is not as easy to see at first, is that Adam and Eve were at war. The enemy declared war on them and they had no idea. They were pawns in his game. This is an important lesson for us. It is by their temptation and sin that we can see the enemy for who he is:

- Never a friend
- Never trustworthy
- Full of false promises
- Deceitful, deceptive and distracting
- Cunning, crafty and conniving

The serpent is a harsh contrast to the love, hope, promises and faithfulness of God. The war wages on and today the slimy, slippery one tries to make you his target. But we are going to dive in right now and learn ways to conquer and overcome his deception. If he wants to be at war - he can be at war with himself – but not with you. Not now. Not ever!

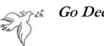 ### Go Deeper...

"The woman was convinced." Genesis 3:6

How often do you let down your defenses or compromise your values because someone tells you something that on some level you want to hear? As women, we tend to be convinced by what we hear around us; and it's even easier to become convinced when it's something we desire. I've considered this is exactly what happened to Eve, particularly after being promised that if she eats it, she will be even more like God whom she loved dearly.

We all long to hear what we want to hear, particularly when our heart and soul is filled with discontent. Even when it appears we have it all, we can find some type of discontent stirring in our soul. Harry S. Truman is credited with saying, "If you can't convince people – confuse them!" This is **exactly** what the enemy did to Eve and to this day he continues his quest to convince and confuse.

So, how do we combat this conniving, deceptive, always-dangling-the-carrot-in-front-of-us enemy? We start by doing exactly what you are doing now: **getting in and staying in God's Word**. This daily communication with God is the armor we need to put on each day to combat the enemy's constant poking of us. Whether you are new to picking up the Bible and studying God's Word, or seasoned in your knowledge of Scripture, the psalms are a great place to start.

The Psalms are filled with songs of praise to remind us of God's mercy, love and provision. If you are feeling discontent in your being, spend some time looking at the following Psalms. Rest here for a few moments. Remember, this is a marathon not a sprint. The days of this study are numbered, but there is no rush or reward to finishing it quickly.

Just rest and allow God to remove any feelings of discontent, jealousy or desire that you may be experiencing. Ask Him to show you a new way to walk in His presence. He will reveal Himself to you, just as He did to Adam and Eve.

Look up and write out the Psalms listed on the following page. What specifically speaks to you in each of these? Put an asterisk near the Psalm that addresses the top need of your heart at this time, and date it.

Psalms to combat deception and the enemy's warfare

Psalm 1 (Remembering Who Watches)
> *I am like a tree flourishing. Living in the blessings of the One who sees me.*

Psalm 16:1, 7-8 (Remembering Who Teaches)
> *Nothing can shake my faith in You, Oh Lord my refuge. I will remain faithful to You.*

Psalm 25 (Remembering Who God is)
> *I trust in God my victor, my hope, my teacher, my guide, my forgiver, and my rescuer!*

Psalm 46:10 (Remembering Who is Forever)
> *Rest easy knowing I Am is with you.*

Psalm 46:1-2, 5 (Remembering Who is our Helper)
> *I need not fall. For God is my ever-present Helper.*

Psalm 91 (Remembering Who Protects us)
> *God loves me, and calls me to rest in Him. He is worthy of my love, trust and praise!*

As you grow in your knowledge of the Word, return to this list and see how God has reconciled with His mercy that which may hold you hostage at this time.

Look beyond these psalms to others that may speak to your heart and refresh and renew your mind. Open to any psalm and you will find encouragement and receive a glimpse of who God is. Write them down and keep them somewhere you will see them throughout your day so you can continue to meditate upon these precious words given to us by God.

3

What's Your Apple?

"A woman is like a tea bag...you can't tell how strong she is until you put her in hot water." Eleanor Roosevelt

She did it. Eve ate the forbidden fruit. Then she handed it to Adam and he ate it too. Tradition tells us Eve ate an apple, but I'm not sure apples grow in the Middle East. Perhaps it was a pomegranate or fig or some exotic fruit I'm not even aware of. However, for our study, we will continue to call this piece of fruit an "apple."

In an instant, the innocence and beauty of the life they were living was gone! They were immediately filled with shame and fear. That is often how sin works. That evening, when God entered the garden to be with them, they did not run to meet Him. Instead, they hid. Imagine God's sadness as He called out to them and they were hiding. This scene makes me weep! They had it all and by one bad decision, they lose everything. Oh, how I believe God is counting the days until He brings all His children home to the Garden of Eden once more for evening walks into eternity!

God knew that Eve would be tempted. He acted as every good Father would. He trained her well in His ways and hoped that when temptation came, she would overcome it. However, she did not. I imagine His pain as He told her the consequences of her sin:

- The pains of pregnancy would be sharpened and in pain she would give birth. (Genesis 3:16)
- She will desire control over her husband, but he will rule over her. (Genesis 3:16)
- They would now toil the land and work for everything they needed to live (Genesis 3:17)

Right now, you might be thinking, "thanks Eve" as you recall your own childbearing pain or struggles with your spouse. Yes, Eve is the mother to more than the generations. She is also the mother to sin. Yet with every sinful act comes an opportunity for redemption. We will look at that too.

I can relate to Eve at this point in her journey. She is a good woman. She is simply a woman trying to figure out her life when sin sneaks up on her. I have had that happen. One moment everything in my world seemed perfect and the next moment I was standing on shaky ground and dealing with the circumstances that sin brought. Yes, sin always gives birth to consequences.

So, let's ponder this a moment as we are reminded how one decision can have consequences that last and affect many. We tread carefully and thoughtfully through this life with God as our compass, our true north. As we continue, we thank Him for His Word that tell us, *"And we know that in all things God works for the good of those who love him, who have been called according to His purpose." (Romans 8:28)* Let this verse provide comfort and hope as you go through today's exercises. God has the power to bring good from anything.

When looking back on your life, what is that one thing that you wish hadn't happened as it did?

Sometimes we may have kept unlikely company. Sometimes by circumstance, we spend time with people we may not have if given the choice. This can be common in work environments. Sometimes we choose to keep company with a certain crowd because we like what they do, how they look or maybe they are the people that tell us what we want to hear.

For some reason, like Eve, we may never be quite satisfied with what is in our reach. We strive for what is just out of our reach. We believe that the apple will be exactly what we need to have the perfect life. At some point in our lives, we each run after our own apples, even if we don't want to admit or recognize it.

What are some of the temptations or apples that you have gone after, or are chasing now?

Have you ever gone after the apple that you thought would bring you peace, happiness and prosperity? (could be a person, place or thing)

When you achieved the apple, how did you feel?

How long did that feeling last?

Were there any people that were hurt while you were pursuing your apple?

Where is this apple today? Do you need to seek forgiveness from God or man because of this apple?

What can you do to ensure that you avoid this temptation in the future?

What strength did you gain from the experience?

Testimony

When I answer these questions honestly, I recall a time in my 20's when I was tempted to use people, particularly men. For example, I would make myself attractive to whatever man I was pursuing, and once I had his interest, I would move on. Yup. Drop him like a hot potato.

Looking back, I believe I did this to fulfill some need within myself. My "apple" was an intense need for the approval of others, particularly men. On the outside I appeared confident, but on the inside, I was very insecure. It was so very tempting to fill the lost and lonely part inside of me with the approval of others. I don't look back on that time often, but when I do it is always reflected upon with a smidge of regret. Those young boys' hearts didn't deserve to be played with! I didn't feel great about it then and I certainly don't now. I recall one poor guy in college who I chased for weeks. Finally, he asked me out on a Thursday night. We had a nice time going to dinner. He was a genuinely nice guy. I went home for the weekend that very next day and broke up with him when I returned to school on Sunday. Yup. The relationship that I chased for weeks, lasted one day. That was just mean. I wish I could even remember his name, but I don't. So, there is no asking him for forgiveness, nor would it be appropriate to even attempt.

One way that I can seek forgiveness for being so self-serving in the past is to act differently today toward the people in my life. I seek to serve rather than receive. I find fulfillment in my relationship with Father, Son and Spirit first, spouse, children, family, friends second: That's the winning ticket! Today, rather than seeking the approval of people, I seek first the approval of God. My goal each day is to live for an audience of One: God and God alone.

Notice I didn't say, "I seek ONLY the approval of God." That is certainly my goal, but I wouldn't be honest if I led you to believe for a second that I had arrived at that goal. Like you, I have moments of greatness when I am solely motivated and inspired by Him. His love and mercy at the root of my every thought and action. Like Eve, when I am fully reliant on Him, there is an ease and excellence to my life. Fear doesn't have a stronghold on me and I can accomplish more than I ever thought possible.
But there are those moments, also like Eve, when my pride and ego rise up and want to take control.

One goal of living a holy life is to be able to recognize the rise in ego, and immediately let go and humble yourself. To live freely in knowing He is in control. To take my hands off the wheel and let Him steer. When we do fall to our apple, you and I need to remember as we look back that there is forgiveness. Perhaps not from the "one date guy" but surely there is forgiveness from the "One and Only I AM." He is the guy that forgives and redeems!

On your knees...

On your knees today, ask God to forgive you for chasing those apples. Eve's life was redeemed and her love for God strengthened through His mercy over her sinful act. Although God was angered by her disobedience, He still covered her in His love and grace. God does that. He did it for Eve and He will do it for you. He brings redemption and new life to some of the darkest corners of our life. It is how His light shines in the darkness and how He lifts us up so we can rise out of the sin and shame and step into that brilliant light of grace and mercy.

When you think about your apple, do you feel as though you are still stuck in your sin and shame? If so, there is no better time than NOW to turn your life over to the care of your loving Father in heaven. If you are still locked in your sin, get on your knees NOW and ask God for his mercy and forgiveness. Ask Him to fill you with a love for Him that is incomprehensible to man. A love for Him that defies logic. Ask Him to fill you with His love, grace and mercy and fill the part of you that you have been feeding with sins that appear to please the flesh. This can show up as food, drink, sexual pleasures, or even an over-active shopping habit. Below write out your request to God. Ask Him to show you the key that will unlock your sin.

Perhaps you have already worked through the pain from your apple. If so, I am going to speculate that when you recall the process you went through, you may discover the key that unlocked your sin was the grace, mercy and love of God through Jesus Christ. For it is only through God's love and grace, the cross of Jesus Christ and gifts of the Holy Spirit that our lives can be completely transformed. Even when we receive forgiveness from other people, it is often their relationship with God that allows them to forgive. God is at the heartbeat of all love and mercy.

Write your prayer of thanksgiving for having received His mercy and grace.

Father, thank You for being the One and Only God who redeems and loves so freely and fully. Bless my sweet friend as she starts to take her hands off the wheel and turns to You to provide the steering for her life. Bless her, as she begins to hand You each of her apples. Lord, help her to see quickly Your hand upon her life. Help her to know that nothing she has ever done is too far gone for Your forgiveness and faithfulness. Help her to experience Your love so she knows deep within that You love her and are with her always.

Go Deeper…

Verse   **REFLECTION**

Psalm 145:8-9
GOD IS GOOD

Ephesians 2:4-10
Saved by Grace

Hebrews 4:16
RECEIVE MERCY AND GRACE

Romans 12:9-18
CHARACTERISTICS TO LIVE BY

1 John 1:9
BE CLEANSED FROM SIN

4

Leadership

"It takes intentional effort to tune out every voice except God's." Henry Blackaby

Leadership. This is a dynamic topic that has been written about and discussed on many platforms. There are many definitions of leadership and countless hours have been spent determining "what makes a great leader" and "who is a great leader." The fact is, as humans, we seek strong leaders.

It's how God created us. **He created us to be followers: followers of Him**. It is why we seek to be under the influence of strong and holy leaders.

Yet in this human form, we often solely seek leaders that are visible and tangible. Society has convinced us that great leaders are born not formed and every few years it seems a new leadership model is the rage. A few styles I continue to notice are:

- The **authoritative** leader: You know, the "do it because I told you to" leader. This leader is power hungry.
- The **coaching and inspiring** leader: the leader who desires to mentor and teach and potentially train up new leaders.

- The **strategic** leader: the leader who is a great thinker and planner.
- The **visionary** leader: the leader who encourages big dreams.
- The **status quo** leader: the leader who doesn't want to rock the boat; the one who was promoted because they were the best member on the team, but they lack leadership.
- The **team-builder leader**: the leader who desires group opinion and consensus.

We can go on and on and on about various types of leaders, but the reality is this: every single person is both a follower and a leader. If you have ever persuaded someone to do something, made a decision that impacted more than one person, followed through on an action, had a job, had children, had a pet – **you are a leader.**

We aren't all paid leaders, but we are leaders and from every leader we can learn something. We can learn what to do and what not to do. It's that simple, really. What we can learn from each other is both how to act and how not to act.

Adam and Eve were the first leaders of humanity. If we focus on their opening scene in Genesis, we might conclude that she is a stronger leader since she exhibited greater influence over Adam and they ate the apple. She got her way. She convinced Adam, as she was convinced by the serpent. For better or worse, she led Adam to sin and to a new life built from the consequences of that decision.

When I put myself in that garden, I see Eve as a pioneer. A woman who has gone where no other woman had gone before. I see a woman who perseveres. Through all of her life's circumstances, she doesn't give up. Let's press into that for a moment.

Eve teaches us a few hard truths about leadership. First, given enough time, every leader can find someone to agree with them. Whether the leader has a good idea or bad idea, they will eventually find someone to corroborate their philosophy. Click on any social media site and type in any topic and you will instantly come in contact with many differing opinions, and each one believing steadfastly they are right. Eve may have been eyeing that apple for some time or it may have been a fleeting fancy, but it wasn't until she had affirmation from another being (that slimy snake) that she decided it was ok to break the rule and go out on a limb (no pun intended).

It is in that moment Eve exercises one type of leadership: she leads us to sin. Sin is an easy place for leaders to visit. Leaders have a responsibility to act within the law and not to think they can rise above it. Leaders have a tremendous effect on the thoughts and actions of those they lead. There is a tremendous responsibility for those placed in leadership positions. The burden of the leader's decisions can weigh heavily and have far-reaching consequences. Eve learned this the hard way.

What I absolutely love about Eve's leadership character, beyond her apple, is that she perseveres, and that perseverance is born from her honesty. When God confronted her, she was honest and said, "The serpent deceived me and I ate." She acknowledged that she was deceived and accepts responsibility for having eaten the apple. This allows God's forgiveness to erase her shame. And she starts over.

She allows herself to be covered in His grace and love. Even though her zip code changes, she remains aligned and in love with her Creator, perhaps more than ever before, because now she understands that the stakes are high.

This is a great lesson for all leaders. All leaders will fail at some point in time. All leaders will face a moment where their world is turned upside down and possibly their zip code changes too. The strategy we can learn from Eve is to keep moving forward. Don't give up and don't give in to sin and pride. Above all, align yourself with God. He is the One we were born to follow. He is our leader. He is the One who can take us on the greatest journey we can imagine.

For all of Eve's heartache, I pray she had double of it in happiness over her lifetime. The very first woman. The first to feel, think, receive, and bear all of it. She was the first. She experienced successes and failures, but through it all, she returns again and again to the Father.

Yes, she led us to sin, but I choose to believe she also led us down the first path of redemption allowing God to bring beauty from ashes.

And that may be the sweetest lesson a leader can teach.

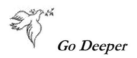

Go Deeper

Finding a Bible Verse

What type of leader do you think Eve is?

Find a scripture verse to sum up your thoughts on Eve's persevering leadership or any other characteristic that is speaking to you as you reflect on this lesson. If you are uncertain where to even start, google the key phrase you are thinking about. A great online resource to help you look through many verses at a time, is www.OpenBible.Info. Click on the "TOPICAL BIBLE" and type in your keyword. Many verses will appear and you can prayerfully go through and determine which speak to you. You will want to look up these verses in your Bible to ensure you are using them in the correct context. For example: Eve as a persevering leader. When I type in "Perseverance" many verses appear. A common theme is not growing weary. Many of these verses could apply to our Eve.[2]

· ·

"Blessed is the one who perseveres under trial because, having stood the test, that person will receive the crown of life that the Lord has promised to those who love him."
James 1:12

5

Redeemed

"Redemption is not perfection. The redeemed must realize their imperfections."
John Piper

Eve had a calling - a very special calling. She was created to be a companion to man, but she had a special calling to create womanhood, in fact, her ultimate calling was to motherhood.

How does God do this? How does he take the woman who gave spiritual birth to the sin of mankind and allow her to give physical birth to every generation?

How? Because God knows your potential and He knows the purpose that each of us are called to. God called Eve to pioneer - to blaze a trail for every woman to follow until the end of time.

Many times, it isn't until years later that we look back and can understand how the circumstances of our lives give birth to a certain plan. I imagine at some point even Eve understood the meaning of her life as she looked in the rearview mirror of her life.

I wonder what it was like in those early days after leaving the physical presence of God. Was Eve the recipient of Adam's resentment and anger at having been banished from the Garden of Eden? I sometimes wonder if he felt the weight of the responsibility to care for this woman while still being angry at her. It's even possible that Adam was ok with blaming Eve for his consumption of the apple. Or, perhaps the encounter with the serpent brought them closer together. We know that in what the enemy desires for chaos and destruction, God can bring forth peace. No matter what emotions were exchanged between them, they were all each other had. Their actions created a new reality for from the time of their banishment until the resurrection of our Savior, God and man were physically separated.

Perhaps there was nothing so dramatic exchanged between them. Since they were the first, they didn't have learned behaviors yet. They weren't taught "how to feel" when someone hurt them. Perhaps they simply walked bravely out of the garden and set about starting their new life and communicating with God in a new way.

We read in Genesis 4:1 that "*Adam lay with his wife Eve, and she became pregnant.*" Do you think Eve understood what it meant to be pregnant or was Eve very confused those nine months as her belly grew and she could feel the pangs of life inside herself? She must have been scared. I often wonder if she prayed to God about it, or at least talked to Adam. I wonder if she thought, "hey – why is my belly growing and his isn't?" Certainly, her heart had to race as she entered childbirth. She might have thought she was dying and paying the highest price for her sin. She may have thought the entire pregnancy to be punishment for her sin. Yet, in that moment after the birth of her son when she held him close and looked him in the eye as her heart swelled with love, she may have felt that special blessing and grace from God that new mothers feel.

For although Eve gave birth to sin we must also remember her as the woman who gave birth to us. This was her calling: to fulfill her God-given purpose of procreation despite the negative effects of her sin. Yes, God can still call us to a mighty purpose even after we have fallen to sin. The very first woman is proof of this secret miracle of His love.

Eve is the first woman to:

- Show courage facing an unknown situation
- Be forgiven and shown mercy by God
- To lead children and teach the ways of the Lord

So what happens next? Eve gives birth to Cain, then his brother Abel. Cain, in Hebrew, means "produce." Abel, translated means "breathless or meaningless." This could be a foreshadowing to the brief life on earth that Abel will experience. For as the brothers presented their crops to the Lord, one brother was favored.

Scripture tells us, *"In the course of time Cain brought some of the fruits of the soil as an offering to the LORD. And Abel also brought an offering—fat portions from some of the firstborn of his flock. The LORD looked with favor on Abel and his offering."* (Gen. 4:3-4)

The story continues that the Lord God accepted Abel's gift, but not Cain's. This angered Cain. God rebuked him by basically saying, "Don't give me some of you, give me the best of you. Give me all of you." This angered Cain more.

Does it anger you? Do you feel like you are doing the right things most of the time and should be rewarded? Many Christians do and yet I encounter many women who tell me that they wish they had more time to spend with God, but they just don't. They believe that showing up for Mass or services on Sunday gives them the key to enter the Kingdom of Heaven.

What about you? Do you think that just showing up to church on Sunday will grant you access to the Kingdom for eternity?

It could. God, in His mercy, will accept whomever He chooses to sit at His heavenly banquet table. But Scripture paints a different picture and if we believe that the Bible is God-breathed and God-inspired, we best take it literally. For example, we are told in Matthew 24:37-44 that we must *keep watch*. We are told that when *the Son of Man returns, that two men will be working together in the field; one will be taken and the other left*. Do you concentrate as Abel did, on bringing your very best to the Lord, or do you believe as Cain did, that your birthright will grant your inheritance of the Kingdom?

Our goal in this life is to be the one God chooses to bring home to His

Kingdom. Right now, if you are having an urging that there is something in your life holding you back from that promise, stop right now and drop to your knees and pray for God to change your heart and your ways to be His heart and His ways.

This is a first step. It is a step that we must sometimes repeat more than once along our journey. Eve had to take this step on several occasions. She teaches us how to be resilient in the ways of the Lord. That's what good leaders do: *they teach us by allowing us to observe them as they walk through all of life's circumstances.*

This isn't the end of the road, however. True freedom in Christ comes when we make a decision to enter into a personal relationship with Him and allow Jesus Christ to become our very life Himself. It is not enough to say that Jesus is the most important thing in our life. No. We must come before Him and proclaim, "Jesus, you ARE my life!"

Remember what happens after the Lord rebuked Cain? Did Cain repent? Did Cain seek God's will? No! He became angrier and more bitter until the moment where he struck the deadly blow to his brother, Abel. He calculated the murder of his brother and he went through with it. Murder in the first degree.

And now another first for Eve: The first woman to grieve the loss of a child.

As we look to Eve, we see:

- a woman of faith and courage
- a woman who had to learn to forgive herself as God forgave her
- a woman who had to persevere without any hint to what the potential outcomes could be
- a woman who trusted that the God who created her would not abandon her, even if she could no longer lay eyes on Him. She knew Him and knew He existed
- a woman redeemed by the birth of a son, Seth – a foreshadowing to the birth of Jesus (Genesis 4:25)

It is with faith and fortitude that we meet our first heroine in the Bible. The first who bore many firsts, Eve.

Go Deeper...

Where are you in the story of Eve? Do you see yourself in any part of her story?

Thank You, Lord, for your mercy and for being the God who redeems. You take our lost, sinful and wounded selves and You mark us with Your Holy Spirit and redeem our lives. Thank You for removing Eve's sin and shame. Thank You for sending Your Son to remove my sin and shame. I praise You that You have been so kind to not have me be remembered for my worst sin the way Eve has been remembered for hers. May we learn from her and grow from her story. I pray this in the name of Your Son, Jesus. Amen.

Life Sentence...

If you were to sum up Eve's life in one sentence, what would it be?

. . . .

...but those who hope in the LORD will renew their strength. They will soar on wings like eagles; they will run and not grow weary, they will walk and not be faint. Isaiah 40:31

Part II

Sarah

6

Called

"Now Sarai was barren; she had no children." Genesis 11:30

Perhaps no other ancient heroine in the Bible so closely resembles the woman of today as Sarah does. From beginning to end, Sarah had to stand against the stereotypes and expectations of her culture. It is impossible to fully study Sarah in a week, so I encourage you to read Genesis 12 through Genesis 23 to further your understanding of this intricate story of the faith-filled Abraham and his leading lady, Sarah.

Her name means "Princess." She is one of the most famed females in the Bible for many reasons, one of them being that Sarah is the great woman supporting a successful man. She is a manager. She manages people and large inventories of livestock and property. She is constantly on the go, quite literally. She supports her husband Abraham in his work and may be the inspiration behind the old adage, "behind every strong man is a stronger woman." Sarah is also Abraham's half-sister. This fact plays an important role in their story. They shared a father, Terah, but had different mothers.

I believe Sarah *knew* God had called her to a special purpose. I choose to believe Abraham shared with her the vision and purpose he received from the Lord. In Genesis 12, just after we meet this God-ordained couple, the Bible describes the moment they were called:

> *"The LORD had said to Abram, "Go from your country, your people and your father's household to the land I will show you.*
>
> *"I will make you into a great nation,*
>   *and I will bless you;*
> *I will make your name great,*
>   *and you will be a blessing.*
> *I will bless those who bless you,*
>   *and whoever curses you I will curse;*
> *and all peoples on earth*
>   *will be blessed through you."*
>
> *So Abram went, as the LORD had told him; and Lot went with him. Abram was seventy-five years old when he set out from Harran. He took his wife Sarai, his nephew Lot, all the possessions they had accumulated and the people they had acquired in Harran, and they set out for the land of Canaan, and they arrived there."*

Wow! The Lord has promised Abraham and Sarah quite a lot in this passage. He is asking a lot from them too, specifically giving them a command to leave everything they have ever known and to start over in a new land.

Oh, how sometimes we wish God would be this specific and clear with us! Yet like us, some days it surely felt impossible for Sarah and Abraham to achieve God's goal. Can you relate to that? Those days when you just want to throw in the towel? Those days when God's promises seem impossible and out of reach? Those moments when, like the Israelites, you feel like you are roaming around the wilderness and the Promised Land is just ahead but out of reach? Sarah must have felt like that although she didn't have the benefit of Moses' story to get her through the way we do.

As I complete the edits of this study which I wrote years ago, I am in such a wilderness. For years I felt God pointing me to a direction, a purpose – my

Promised Land. Yet before we reach our God-appointed destination, we often spend time in the wilderness just as the Israelites did after Moses freed them from Pharaoh's rule. The journey the Israelites were going on should have taken them eleven days, yet the Lord allowed them to roam the wilderness for forty years until they had learned all that He desired for them to learn in preparation for stepping into their Promised Land *in faith*.

I'm in that wilderness. Ten months ago, after ten years of supporting my husband and his debilitating neurological and psychological health, we had to make the decision to place him in assisted living. At the age of fifty-nine, we could no longer keep him safe at home. For a decade, his care was the focus of our family. Our children grew up knowing, caring and loving a sick father. We were blessed with the generous kindness of many over the years who came to help during unplanned overnight trips to the emergency department, hospitalizations to re-learn how to walk, talk, chew and swallow and much more. At that time, I thought I was in the wilderness. I wasn't. I was in Egypt under Pharaoh's rule.

These last ten months had me wandering aimlessly. Confused, bewildered and praying for provision in the same way the Israelites asked for manna, quail and water. (Exodus 16 – 17) Yet, I know that God will deliver me into the Promised Land He has purposed for me. It is a matter of time and can come quickly with my willingness to step out in faith to meet Him there.

Perhaps you can relate to this. God may have placed a dream or promise in your heart the way He did for Sarah and Abraham and you are waiting in faithful hope until it comes to pass. If so, I'm glad our paths are crossing at this exact moment. I pray you draw the same comfort from pressing in and placing yourself within these stories of the Bible. I pray these men and women come alive for you and you can learn the secret truths that God has in store for you in the secret places. Sarah gets a few mentions by name in the New Testament. In fact, Sarah's name is the most widely mentioned female name in the entire Bible. I think Sarah reminds me of women today because like us, she makes mistakes. Like Eve, she tries to rush God's timing and it doesn't work out so well for her or for the other woman or for those around them. As we study Sarah, once again, we will see how disobedience and inserting our will ahead of God's will has far-reaching consequences.

We meet Sarah in the eleventh of chapter of Genesis verses 27-32:

> *27 This is the account of Terah's family line.*
>
> *Terah became the father of Abram, Nahor and Haran. And Haran became the father of Lot. 28 While his father Terah was still alive, Haran died in Ur of the Chaldeans, in the land of his birth. 29 Abram and Nahor both married. The name of Abram's wife was Sarai, and the name of Nahor's wife was Milkah; she was the daughter of Haran, the father of both Milkah and Iskah. 30 Now Sarai was childless because she was not able to conceive.* (emphasis added)

In this passage, we quickly learn a few things about this Sarah: 1) she is married to Abraham; and 2) she is unable to bear children.

What an introduction. Defined for all time as "unable to bear children." Even our ancient sister was defined by the world before being defined by God. We can relate to this as cultures define people based on traditions and beliefs rather than character.

Before we even begin to study Sarah, we need to learn a few truths about the Ancient Jewish culture. The following information was taken from the website WomenintheAncientWorld.com.

> *The Ancient Hebrew law code outlined in the Bible unfortunately lacks the detail that can be found in other ancient legal systems such as the Babylonian and Roman, but we can at least summarize the general principles.*
>
> • *Marriage was called "taking a wife." Marriage involved sexual intercourse.*
>
> • *While there was no death penalty in Hebrew law for property crimes, adultery was a capital [offense] for both participants.*
>
> • *Marriage and children were necessary to have a fulfilled life. A childless woman could call herself a mother by giving her maid-servant to her husband as a second wife, assuming of course, the servant did indeed produce a child.*
>
> • *A widow had the right to marry her husband's brother if he lived in the same town.*

○ *Polygyny (plural marriage) was permitted but uncommon.*

○ *Divorce was easy for a man and impossible for a woman.*

• *Childlessness was the most common reason for divorce.*

• *The woman moved to the husband's home and family.*

• *While the husband was clearly the boss, each expected love from the other and a wife had the legal right to (financial) support.*

Throughout the Ancient World having many children was thought to be a good thing. Society could not survive without a new generation to take over, and the individual did not want to face old age or ill health without a family to provide care and support.

Sons were preferred for two very good reasons: males had control of the wealth, and in a patrilocal society where the bride moved to the husband's home sons expanded the family while daughters were dispersed into the society at large. For all these reasons, neighbors tended to feel sorry for families without children and to favor families with children, especially sons. A childless woman who was wealthy enough to own a maid-servant had an interesting option: she could give her maid to her husband and claim any resulting child as her own. Childless women without maid-servants were likely to find themselves divorced.[3]

Wow, that is a lot of pressure! Sarah was most likely put down because of her inability to conceive. My guess is that few would be brave enough to treat her that way in front of her husband, Abraham, but when he wasn't around, all bets were off. Women often have targets on their backs where arrows of discontent, disagreement and jealousy are aimed. It was most likely no different for Sarah. She was a woman who had position in life and she managed it well. Her one flaw in the world's eyes? Childless.

As a woman who has not given biological birth to her children (my treasures are both adopted), I am feeling Sarah's pain. I can't imagine living in a world where I was judged on my ability to conceive or not conceive.

Testimony

My husband's Italian grandmother lived from 1894-1975. Grandma Rosie came to the United States on a boat when she was 16 years old. She was pregnant and wanted to be sure that her child was born in America. Rosie and her husband settled in an Italian neighborhood in South Philadelphia where, for the next thirty years, she was ridiculed and told she only had "one eye" because she only had one child. She suffered extreme mental anguish and was mocked and scolded...*all because she only had ONE child?* **Poor Rosie!**

Unbelievable! To think that these beliefs continued to exist. When her "one eye" became a doctor, married and had four children, Rosie was vindicated! Yes. Vindication came when the world said, "You are now special – your only son is a doctor and he has four eyes – four children." Sigh!

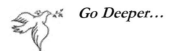 ### *Go Deeper...*

Where is your worth?

People can be cruel. Women can be cruel. Women treating other women badly is, unfortunately, quite common. The girls at work, the moms from your kids' teams, sometimes life feels like a perpetual middle school classroom. We are judged by our looks rather than our abilities; our property rather than our character; and who we married rather than who we are.

Let's pause a moment from the world and its hold on us and reflect on this truth: God, Himself, sent His only Son that whoever may believe would have eternal life.

Like Eve...like Sarah...like Rosie...we need to take our worth from God – not from a world that will deceive us and lie to us. The world is jealous of God's army. It doesn't understand the faith that pours out through the Body of Christ and therefore the world and the enemy in the world seek to destroy that which they don't understand.

When have you made a decision based on the world's view rather than God's view?

How did that decision impact your life? Did it impact your future? Do you ever look back on that decision with regret? With resentment? Did that decision harden your heart toward another person or Almighty God Himself?

There is Good News!!! God can use all of you, even your flaws and failings, to exert His purpose for your life. Never give up because *God never gives up on you*. Sarah laughed at God and yet God loved her and helped her fulfill her purpose: to bear an heir that would serve the generations and whose ultimate lineage would bear the Son of Man.

There is no shame or condemnation in Christ Jesus! Once you have accepted Him, you are graced to begin a new life as a new creation in Him. And the best part? God can and will use all the sticky areas of your life for a holy purpose. His Word tells us so in Romans 8:28,

> *28 And we know that in all things God works for the good of those who love him, who have been called according to his purpose.* Romans 8:28

This verse is your shield, protecting you from ever thinking you are a lost cause. Protecting you from ever believing that your life doesn't matter or is hopeless. God can redeem, fix and elevate anyone! Even Sarah, even you and me. Be steadfast in believing God for who He is. He is above all, loving to those who love Him and He can take any mess and bless it.

7

Who's Timing?

"Trust in God's timing. It's better to wait awhile and have things fall into place, than to rush and have things fall apart." Author Unknown

Sarah was growing impatient at the seemingly lack of fulfillment of God's plan. Imagine yourself being promised the one thing you have waited a lifetime for. Perhaps it is a holy spouse, a position of leadership or, like Sarah, a baby. Spending time in the waiting room of our lives, is one of the hardest, most difficult things to do for many of us.

Today is all about timing, our timing and God's timing. How often we seem to be operating on different timetables than God. If things are difficult, we want resolution swiftly. We want the pain to be quick and brief, if at all. We do not like prolonged illnesses, prolonged divorces, prolonged financial struggles and in Sarah's case, prolonged infertility.

Sarah's issue with infertility is what ultimately leads her, and us, to meeting Hagar, the "other woman."

Don't we all have the other woman in our life? The other woman comes in all shapes and sizes, and not every other woman is an enemy. Let's use the acronym OW for the Other Woman. No coincidence there. (OW!) A few examples of the OW could be:

- The woman we wish to emulate
- The woman we are slightly envious of
- The woman who seems prettier, smarter, and wields more influence
- The woman who stole our boyfriend or husband
- The woman who was promoted ahead of us

Yes, since the beginning of time, or at least since Sarah and Hagar, there has always been the Other Woman.

What do you think God wishes for us when we are looking at the other woman? What do you think He hopes our heart song to be when we are facing, in our minds, a female opponent?

Perhaps the OW in your life is a colleague who wields her power in a negative way, or a neighbor who takes up your afternoons filling your home and head with gossip?

Yes...for every type of female there is another type - the other woman.

Yet, I believe God may put some of these women in our life for a reason. Oh, I can hear some of you already - "Just stop it, Michele. There are some women out there who are just plain nasty and evil. Why would God put them in my life?" Yes. You are right. The world is filled with mean girls. I know a few myself. By way of brokenness and betrayal they have come to believe the only way they can survive is to act tough or to fight. They have lost the softness and sensitivity of their womanhood. They are angry, bitter and always seem to be looking for an argument and have a penchant for proving themselves right.

But I still believe God is whispering to us, "I have put these women in your life for a reason!" From these women, we learn two very important lessons: how to behave and how not to behave.

Could this be the reason for the other woman? Could this be why God is putting a Hagar in your life? Possibly. But let's entertain another thought. Perhaps these antagonists in our life actually play a holy role in our formation.

God knows you. He knows your faithfulness. He knew Sarah's faithfulness. God trusts you. He sees you and He may just believe that out of all the women in the world, YOU have been chosen by HIM to pray for and be an example to that OTHER WOMAN.

Hagar didn't change from the inside out until she encountered the Lord. We must pray for the Other Woman in our life, pray she has her own magnificent, personal encounter with Jesus. He alone has the power to save and perfect her.

Yes...we must pray for her:

- We must pray she turns from the world and seeks God with all her heart.

- We must pray she finds her worth in the Word and not her worth in every person she meets and what they think of her.

- We must pray she finds her worth in who God says she is and not in her title or her power.

We must pray. Jesus even says to us, *"Love your enemies and pray for your persecutors."* (Matthew 5:44)

We must pray for her. And perhaps, somewhere, there is a woman out there who thinks you are too pretty, too important, too together, or too powerful...and she is praying for you. Yes, each and every day we can be Sarah, or we can be Hagar. Both loved by God. Both chosen by God.

And remember this: to Hagar, Sarah was the other woman. Sarah was the woman who had it all. Sarah had the husband, influence and control of the household matters. Sarah was the woman who made a decision that changed the course of Hagar's life. It's simply a matter of perspective and in reading this passage from scripture, we can agree that both women were right and both women were wrong in their actions.

So, pray. Pray for your Sarahs and pray for your Hagars. In fact, pause right now and write out the name of a particular woman (or women) you can begin holding in prayer.

As we look at the dynamic between Sarah and Hagar, we see their relationship can be defined as difficult at best.

I have always wondered if each time Sarah looked at Hagar she saw Pharaoh and was reminded of the struggles in Egypt. Jewish tradition and many Rabbinical scholars teach Hagar was Pharaoh's daughter and he gave her to Sarah and Abraham because he believed them to be righteous. It is asserted that Pharaoh said, "It is better that my daughter should be a slave in the house of such a woman, than a mistress in another house." Ironic that Hagar becomes both slave and mistress. Perhaps for a time having Hagar in their home plagued Sarah's thoughts. It is more likely that Sarah continued to show Hagar the same respect she did in the King's house, where she treated Hagar well. Sarah was kind. Sarah, we have learned, also took everything to God. Every desire, every heartache, every concern.

Because of the culture at that time suggesting a woman without child could build up her family through her maid-servant, it is no surprise that Sarah offers Hagar to Abraham. I can just imagine the thoughts in her head, "Perhaps, Lord, *this is the reason* you sent us to Egypt. I was to come back with Hagar and *she is the one* who will conceive the child that will give birth to the generations as you have promised Abraham and I." It's plausible Sarah would have such a passing thought. The situation can certainly be justified like that. It makes perfect sense, right? We see how easy it could have been for Sarah to rationalize that Hagar is part of God's plan.

 ### *Go Deeper...*

My way or His way?

What we don't know is what the circumstances were leading up to the decision to hand Hagar over to Abraham. Here are a few possibilities:

- Had Sarah just endured more anguish and ridicule from her countrymen? Let's face it, a beautiful woman with a great husband is a target for abuse and gossip by other women. Could this have been her breaking point?

- Could Sarah have caught a playful exchange between Abraham and another woman, and she thought if she offered him her maidservant then at least she would still have some power in the game?
- Had she simply deemed that enough time had passed and if she was going to be the one to give Abraham his child, it would have happened by now?

These scenarios are quite plausible, and we can understand how each one could affect Sarah's decision to take action. There is only one thing missing as far as I can tell, and that one thing is God. Scripture doesn't tell us where or when Sarah took this matter up with God. She had to have cried out to Him many times. There is no doubt about that. But this actual decision to give Hagar to Abraham, did she speak to God about this, or did she act as Eve did, quickly and ultimately in disobedience pushing her own will and agenda in a moment of weakness?

I believe if Sarah had taken this request prayerfully, and in faith to God, He would have intervened for her as He did in Egypt. It's likely that Sarah acted out of her own feelings and frustration rather than on faith.

We do this too, don't we? We take our laundry list of prayer requests to God and if He doesn't answer in our timing, we step in to fix it ourselves. I know I did this many times as I waited for a miracle of wholeness to heal my husband. For over a decade, we battled his depression and neurological decline. Often, I would step out and make decisions based on my feelings rather than my faith. We all want our life to be without drama. As a result, we often seek comfort and security and when any event or person threatens that, it can be difficult to wait for God's most perfect and holy intervention.

There is a very important lesson in this story for all of us:

Impossible difficulties cannot be resolved by human intervention.

God alone can see the need and miraculously provide.

When have you been faced with an impossible difficulty that could not be resolved by human intervention?

Did you reach a point while waiting where you were confident God, alone, would resolve your situation?

Since then, have you taken every request up with your Heavenly Father, or have you slipped, as Sarah did, back into the habit of relying on your own timing, will and logic?

As we can already see from our study, God's answer often looks different than what we expect. Has this ever happened in your life? What did you learn about the Sovereignty of God and his love for you?

On your knees...

Ask God to help you to remember to bring all requests to Him in prayer, petition and thanksgiving *before* you make any decisions and *before* you set things in motion. Ask Him to send you a billboard and to walk with you through every decision big and small.

"Do not be anxious about anything, but in every situation, by prayer and petition, with thanksgiving, present our requests to God. And the peace of God, which transcends all understanding will guard your hearts and mind in Christ Jesus." Philippians 4:6-7

8

Consequences & Relationships

"Leave the broken irreversible past in God's hands and step into the invincible future with Him." Oswald Chambers

Sarah demonstrates for us, our inclination to take matters into our own hands, rather than wait for God's resolution. Let's face it, Sarah is quite literally, not getting any younger. Culture approves that the woman of the house could become a mother through a surrogate, so why not Hagar?

Knowing the culture of the day and the pressure mounting on Sarah to have Abraham's baby – the promised, holy son of Israel- we can rationalize why she made the decision she did.

Hagar is Sarah's slave, in fact her name means "Stranger." She had few, if any, rights. She was a woman, a foreigner and a servant. She has no one to advocate for her. She is at the mercy of others. She is handed over to sleep with Abraham and she finds herself pregnant with his child. This must have been very bittersweet for Sarah. I'm hopeful she put her best face forward and supported and even nurtured Hagar.

As the story unfolds, it is written:

> *When she knew she was pregnant, she began to despise her mistress.5 Then Sarai said to Abram, "You are responsible for the wrong I am suffering. I put my slave in your arms, and now that she knows she is pregnant, she despises me. May the LORD judge between you and me."*
>
> *6 "Your slave is in your hands," Abram said. "Do with her whatever you think best."*

For Hagar, it wasn't bitter-sweet. It was only bitter. She was angry. She was now pregnant with a child that she hadn't asked for. She was away from her family and her land. Perhaps she dreamed of the day that Abraham would take her as his wife. Perhaps she would become the favored wife rather than Sarah? Yes, her daydreams may have been filled with happiness and hope. Yet, when her life didn't take shape that way, she reacted in resentment and bitterness toward Sarah.

Suddenly this story is filled with envy, resentment and pride. This won't be the last time that God's chosen people struggle to deal with the consequences created by their own willful decisions. If only Sarah had persevered in faith. But she did not. If only **we** would persevere in faith…yet we rarely do.

Sarah was now faced with a different type of uncertainty: Would she lose her place as first wife? Let's face it, Abraham denied her before. In Egypt he demoted her position from wife to sister. *Would he do that again?*

Sarai or Sarah? Abram or Abraham?

There are several references in Scripture to God changing the name of His people. This name change typically coincides with their fully committing their life to Him.

The same happens for us. When we commit to the Lord, we receive a new identity, a new purpose in Him. More than a name change, our entire life blossoms and changes into beautiful destiny.

Dear friend, I am simply speculating because what I see here is a woman who is now making decisions based on her feelings rather than her faith. I wonder what the exchange was like between these two women. What was the breaking point that brought about Hagar's banishment?

Scripture tells us, *"Then Sarai mistreated Hagar; so she fled from her."* (Genesis 16:6) Were there harsh words between Sarah and Hagar? Was Hagar so angry with Sarah that she began to undermine her authority or disobey her? Did she begin to waste time and resources? Or, did she turn lazy, as she was now pregnant? Did Hagar insist on being pampered herself? Or, perhaps Hagar remained a faithful servant and the entire conflict was born in Sarah's mind out of jealousy.

Did Sarah become verbally abusive? Scripture doesn't go into the details, but what we know is that it became so bad that it began to affect Sarah's relationship with Abraham. Abraham appears to grow weary of Sarah's constant complaining and nagging when he finally chastised her by saying, "Handle it yourself."

Sarah handles it the way many of us handle problems: She strikes back. She strikes with a sharp tongue and begins to make Hagar's life miserable.

As women, we often strike out when we become threatened or intimidated, and the weapon of choice is typically the tongue. We speak sharply. We begin to gossip. Perhaps we even allude to mistruths that begin to spread lies about the other person. Yes, Sarah no doubt struck with her tongue. She probably also struck with her power. Perhaps she reserved the toughest, dirtiest work for Hagar, treating her so poorly that Hagar believed her best option was to flee.

Have you ever done that? Have you ever used your power or position to negatively impact someone else? Power and position as defined in your role as mother, wife, daughter, sister, friend, co-worker, boss, etc.....?

Have you ever acted out as Hagar did and allowed your daydreams to affect your reality?

Have you ever acted out as Sarah did? Manipulating others to do your will and then becoming angry and resentful of the result? What happened and ultimately what were the consequences? Perhaps this happened to you, but you were the Hagar?

Because here is where it gets really good! All the pain that Hagar felt…the being used…the being mistreated…all of that, *all of it* led to an encounter with the Lord!!! B-I-N-G-O! Hagar receives a visit from the Lord himself. He, Himself saves her from death in the desert.

Doesn't this so typically represent God's economy? The lesser one by social standards, the one who struggles, *receives the personal encounter with God?*

Yes. Because God loves each of us the same. None more. None less. Tough to accept sometimes, but it is the way it is. Truth. It is why Jesus taught us to love one another and pray for our persecutors. In the eyes of the Father, we are equally loved.

Scholars believe that the "angel of the Lord" was probably a manifestation of God (theophany) or a Christophany, an appearance of the pre-incarnate Messiah. Scripture continues:

> *7 The angel of the LORD found Hagar near a spring in the desert; it was the spring that is beside the road to Shur. 8 And he said, "Hagar, slave of Sarai, where have you come from, and where are you going?"*
>
> *"I'm running away from my mistress Sarai," she answered.*
>
> *9 Then the angel of the LORD told her, "Go back to your mistress and submit to her." 10 The angel added, "I will increase your descendants so much that they will be too numerous to count."*
>
> *11 The angel of the LORD also said to her:*
>
> *"You are now pregnant and you will give birth to a son. You shall name him Ishmael,[a] for the LORD has heard of your misery. 12 He will be a wild donkey of a man, his hand will be against everyone and everyone's hand against him, and he will live in hostility toward all his brothers."*
>
> *13 She gave this name to the LORD who spoke to her: "You are the God who sees me," for she said, "I have now seen the One who sees me."14 That is why the well was called Beer Lahai Roi; it is still there, between Kadesh and Bered.*

15 So Hagar bore Abram a son, and Abram gave the name Ishmael to the son she had borne. 16 Abram was eighty-six years old when Hagar bore him Ishmael.

The angel of the Lord speaks with authority and told Hagar to return to her mistress and *submit to her authority,* saying *"I will give you more descendants than you can count."* Hagar obeyed. She submitted to the Word of the Lord and to the authority over her on this earth, Sarah and Abraham.

The Lord told Hagar to name the child Ishmael which means "God hears" since the Lord heard her crying in the desert. He also warned that Ishmael would be a *"wild man, as untamed as a wild donkey. He will raise his fist against everyone and everyone will be against him. He will live in open hostility against all his relatives."* Yet Hagar responds obediently to the Lord. She calls Him *El Roi* "the God who sees me" because she learned on that very day the omnipotence of God and the reign that He has over all our lives.

This is a very personal and powerful message to all of us. God SEES you. He sees everything about you: your soul and your heart. He understands you. You are not disposable or dispensable and neither was Hagar. We may be able to hide from others but we cannot hide from Him. You are seen as Hagar was seen. Each is His own beloved.

As I am completing the editing of this study, I find myself messaging back and forth with a dear friend one winter Saturday afternoon. Susan and I met at a weekend women's retreat and became quick friends and Bible study partners. Our texts and emails move fluidly between real life talk and Bible study talk. She is smart, funny, super-cute and has that great Maine accent that drops all her r's. She has a heart for teaching women and children and her testimony bears witness to how our merciful, loving God can bring beauty even out of the darkest moments of our lives.

Yesterday as we are texting back and forth, Susan begins raising questions about Sarah, Abraham and Hagar's relationship. Susan had been preparing a teaching on 1 Peter, chapter three which begins:

"Wives, in the same way submit yourselves to your own husbands so that, if any of them do not not believe the word, they may be won over without words by the behaviors of their wives."

Verses five and six go on to say,

"For this is the way the holy women of the past who put their hope in God used to adorn themselves. They submitted themselves to their own husbands, like Sarah who obeyed Abraham and called him her lord."

This got Susan thinking and questioning if Hagar felt bullied having been submitted to both Abraham and Sarah. Interesting thought, but I questioned our putting a twenty-first century social behavior on an ancient society. Back then, as we have discussed, what Sarah and Abraham did was within the letter of the law. As my sweet Susan dug deeper into reading and studying about this triad relationship of old, God revealed to her a powerful truth that expresses exactly what we can learn from looking back.

Hagar went from daughter of Pharaoh to slave and then to outcast when Sarah banished her until she encountered Jesus in the desert. We go from being a slave in our sin and being cast out by our sin and choices to being daughter of the Most High when we encounter this man Jesus.

Hagar: daughter to slave

Us: slave to daughter

Holy wow!

 **Go Deeper...**

There is a crazy juxtaposition that has occurred in the story now: Hagar appears to be found in the favor of God, while Sarah is repenting for her disobedience. Sarah had to have been beside herself when Hagar left. Imagine having to tell Abraham, "by the way, the lady carrying your baby, the promised one? She ran off..." It could not have been a good time for Sarah.

This story teaches us a few things:

1) Walk, think and act in faith; God's timing is perfect.

2) When you are wronged, do not speak out in anger (this relates to the New Law that Jesus taught, "love one another and pray for your persecutors". (Matthew 5:44)

3) God seeks to love and forgive all His children. Our birthright is in Him.

4) God hears and sees us in our cry for help.

For a while after Ishmael is born, we can surmise that Sarah and Abraham tried to live amicably with Hagar and Ishmael and did their best to assist with raising the child. I believe it is this faithfulness to God that allows for their redemption of the past and for God to continue doing His mighty work in them.

We see again in Genesis 18 where Sarah's disbelief earns her a chastisement from the Lord. She laughs as she overhears the three holy visitors telling Abraham that *this time next year, Sarah your wife will have a son.* (Genesis 18:10) Sarah attempts to deny her behavior, but *the God who sees, has seen!* Sarah must have had a large of piece of humble pie that day, but it appears by all accounts that this was the day that she became fully invested in trusting the Lord and in His perfect timing. For the humbling that she received, she equally must have been filled with hope: *She would be conceiving a son within the year!*

Sarah is now **prepared** to conceive and raise this boy. She has **surrendered to the One, true, holy and living God. She is now walking by faith and not by feelings.** God takes her misguidedness and makes a miracle.

And the woman conceives.

9

His Will, My Way

In the story of Eve, we considered several types of positive leadership models that are still widely used today. However, in the story of Sarah, we see another very common leadership style. In fact, Frank Sinatra wrote a song about it. It's called, "I did it my way!"

The "I did it my way" or "control-freak" leader is often born out of a necessity to solve problems. To the plus side, we could call this "taking action" leadership. That is exactly what we see with Sarah. Page after page of Scripture describes Sarah's knack for problem solving.

I can hear Sarah's encouragement and suggestions to Abraham throughout their story.

> "God is calling us to a new land? No problem! Let's get the animals and family together and set out at once. You gather up the men. I will gather the women and children. We will gather the grain and the weavings. Let's meet back here in two hours!"

"You think Pharaoh may kill you because I am your wife and he may want me for himself? No problem! Let's tell him I'm your sister. It's not a lie!"

"It's been ten years since God told us we would have a child. Why don't we use my maid Hagar to carry our promised child? Go sleep with her!"

Now, I'm certainly not trying to make light of any of these situations. These were difficult, dangerous events that occurred in Sarah's life. However, I think we can make the point that Sarah is a leader who is willing to act. She knows her place. She understood her influence over Abraham and her position as his wife. She was willing to set things into motion to achieve a result.

This can be a great quality for a leader: the willingness to take initiative. This is an important quality and one that most would agree is looked upon highly. Followers want to follow people who lead. Teams want a decisive manager. Companies benefit from a leader who is willing to act. However, there is a downside to this type of leadership. If the motives of the leader are not pure, or are not aligned with the will of God, self-serving decisions can be made that can negatively impact the group.

Unfortunately, we see some of this in Sarah's story as well. She was looking for a means to the end. This is not very different from the boss or co-worker you know who is only interested in moving paper off their desk rather than performing the job correctly. They are simply interested in getting it done. Sarah knew God's promise was for a baby so by golly she was going to make sure there was a baby! She was going to do what God was clearly not doing. Yet.

In *The Maxwell Leadership Bible* by John C. Maxwell, the leadership author describes Sarah's leadership in the following way. On page twenty, Mr. Maxwell so brilliantly writes the following:

She illustrates what happens when an insecure leader tries to work independently of God. Insecure leaders:

- *Believe God is inattentive, absent or even against them.*

- *Allow their circumstances to determine their understanding of God's character.*
- *See life through a perspective of scarcity rather than abundance.*
- *Become self-seeking and manipulative.*
- *Feel intimidated and deal with others through intimidation.*
- *Resent the success of others and angrily turn on them.*
- *Think that if one person succeeds, someone else must lose.*
- *Blame others for their dilemma.*
- *See themselves as martyrs.*
- *Conclude that attempts at control seem more logical than trusting God.*[4]

John Maxwell provides this very detailed, spot-on and important list of the characteristics we note in Sarah and other leaders that force their will, their way.

We can look at this list and see Sarah's story throughout it. Did she believe that God couldn't accomplish this? Had she grown so weary from all her years of waiting? She was *intimidated* when Hagar got pregnant and then dealt with Hagar through *intimidation*. She *resented* Hagar's success. Sarah wanted to "win" and therefore Hagar had to "lose." She *blames* Abraham for the whole situation and she sees herself as a *righteous martyr* in the story. Her behavior tells us, as John Maxwell concludes, that *"attempts at her controlling the situation seemed more logical than trusting God."*[5]

Well, I don't know about you, but I can take this same list and apply it to my life. There are times when I have been angry with God because He seemed inattentive to my needs. I have imposed my circumstances on God and believed Him to be a certain way because of them. (Why is He punishing me? What did I do to deserve anything but His love?) I haven't been a big one on intimidation, although that's my perspective, others may disagree.

Then, like Sarah, I was humbled. Really. Really. Humbled. Down low. I recall a time in prayer, when I came before the Lord in anger over my relationship with my husband. Although there was a physical reason for his behavior, I couldn't see that. I could only see that he was neglecting the kids and me and not participating in his family the way I wanted. *"Lord, this man needs a change of heart. He needs a heart transplant!"* Imagine my surprise, when I felt my own words come crashing down on me when the Lord responded, *"You are the one who needs the heart transplant."* I had not been as loving or merciful as I would like to think. I had been prescribing to a righteous attitude. It takes one time to receive a humbling like Sarah did (and like I did) to start to peel away at the "control freak" leadership that we can all subscribe to at one point or another.

I had stopped leading in the most important relationship in my life. I was trying to control the people closest to me. I was pushing my agenda and my wants on the circumstances and I wasn't stopping to count the cost.

This is the heart of Sarah's lesson to us on leadership: If the motives of the leader are not pure, or are not aligned with the will of God, self-serving decisions can be made that will negatively impact the group.

On the other hand, **when a leader seeks to go low and remain humbled, God has the room and space to perform absolute miracles.** His will can be accomplished through the lowliest among us, if we have but a humble and willing heart. Like Sarah, God used these moments of humility for me to return to Him. I could literally feel myself turning toward the Son, seeking repentance and grace.

 Go Deeper...

Let's Get Real

Reflecting on John Maxwell's list of Sarah's leadership qualities, can you see any areas of your life where you have been operating from a place of control or lack of trust?

Do you find yourself returning to this type of mentality, or has a major humbling cured you of the "control-freak" leadership model?

Throughout every Gospel, Jesus' teaching on humility is very clear. Imagine being on the hillside listening to the carpenter's son preaching words and themes you had never heard before. Here, standing among the people is the Son of God. Talk about leadership! God literally showed up to lead His people! Jesus came to personally model the idea of *servant leadership*. The servant leader is servant first. Serving others is the primary motivation and leading them is secondary. In fact, to a true servant leader, leadership is a result of the service. It is not what the servant leader necessarily sets out to do.

Leadership is unique and personal to each. We can observe and study winning philosophies and behaviors, but good leaders look to the ones they are leading to determine how best to serve them.

In each of the four Gospels, Jesus shows us His seriousness on the idea of humility. Take a few moments and look up the following Scripture passages.

- What is Jesus speaking to you in each of these stories?
- Is He preaching a same or similar message in each of these examples?
- How can you apply these lessons to your own life and leadership style?

Matthew 25: 31-40

> *"When the Son of Man comes in his glory, and all the angels with him, he will sit on his glorious throne.* *32 All the nations will be gathered before him, and he will separate the people one from another as a shepherd separates the sheep from the goats.* *33 He will put the sheep on his right and the goats on his left.*

34 Then the King will say to those on his right, 'Come, you who are blessed by my Father; take your inheritance, the kingdom prepared for you since the creation of the world. 35 For I was hungry and you gave me something to eat, I was thirsty and you gave me something to drink, I was a stranger and you invited me in, 36 I needed clothes and you clothed me, I was sick and you looked after me, I was in prison and you came to visit me.'

37 Then the righteous will answer him, 'Lord, when did we see you hungry and feed you, or thirsty and give you something to drink? 38 When did we see you a stranger and invite you in, or needing clothes and clothe you? 39 When did we see you sick or in prison and go to visit you?'

40 The King will reply, 'Truly I tell you, whatever you did for one of the least of these brothers and sisters of mine, you did for me." (Emphasis added)

Mark 9:33-37

33 "They came to Capernaum. When he was in the house, he asked them, "What were you arguing about on the road?" 34 But they kept quiet because on the way they had argued about who was the greatest.

35 Sitting down, Jesus called the Twelve and said, "Anyone who wants to be first must be the very last, and the servant of all." (Emphasis added)

36 He took a little child whom he placed among them. Taking the child in his arms, he said to them, 37 "Whoever welcomes one of these little children in my name welcomes me; and whoever welcomes me does not welcome me but the one who sent me."

Luke 22:24-27

24 "A dispute also arose among them as to which of them was considered to be greatest. 25 Jesus said to them, "The kings of the Gentiles lord it over them; and those who exercise authority over them call themselves Benefactors. 26 But you are not to be like that. Instead, the greatest among you should be like the youngest, and the one who rules like the one who serves. 27 For who is greater, the one who is at the table or the one who serves? Is it not the one who is at the table? But I am among you as one who serves." (Emphasis added.)

John 3:30

30 "He must become greater; I must become less."

On your knees...

Oh, sweet Jesus! Time and again you tell me through Your Word that I must go low and humble myself. Help me, Lord, to be one who serves, one who submits and one who surrenders. In Your holy and precious name. Amen.

10

Redeemed

As we wrap up our study on Sarah, please open your Bible and read Genesis chapter 20.

Abimelech means "my father the king." It was a title of authority and respect given that was very similar to that of Pharaoh. This chapter is Egypt déjà vu. Abraham and Sarah moved on to Gerar (twelve miles south of Gaza – yes, this was taking place close to what we know today as the Gaza Strip). The Bible tells us that "living there as a foreigner" Abraham again decides for their safety to introduce Sarah as his sister, not wife. We must remember, that this was always done as a tool for protection over their personal safety. As brother, Abraham could still offer protection over Sarah. If he had been murdered because the rulers desired Sarah for themselves, she would have had no protection as a widow.

I want to share a description with you that comes directly out of my New Living Translation Study Bible (NLT). The study notes around verses 1-18 on page 60 read:

> *"This second 'sister story' in Genesis occurred shortly before Sarah became pregnant with Isaac. On both occasions (in Egypt, and now in*

Gerar) God protected Abraham and Sarah's marriage in purity for the sake of the covenant promises. Participation in God's plan requires separation from **worldly corruption.** *This story took place in the Promised Land; it showed Israel how God intervened in people's lives to fulfill his plan, how God continued to protect them against threats from other tribes and how God used his chosen people to mediate his relationship with the nations. God's preventing the destruction of Abraham's marriage by adultery reminded the Israelites to keep their marriages morally and radically pure."* (Emphasis added)[6]

We must believe after this Abraham and Sarah themselves felt completely ready to accept God's promise. It certainly feels as though the time has come for them to step into their purpose. Sodom and Gomorrah have been destroyed. Their marriage was saved once again and it feels as though the world has undergone a bit of a purification, paving the way for the birth of Isaac.

My dear friend and Christian author Deborah Lovett always reminds me that every story, every life, is an example of a birth, death and resurrection. This is certainly true in Sarah's story.

Birth – Chosen by God

Sarah believed in God's covenant with her husband Abraham. She knew she was chosen for a special purpose for as Abraham's wife, she would surely bear the heir that allowed Abraham to be father of all nations. Sarah worked diligently in obscurity. She worked hard to always have her home be welcoming and hospitable. This was no easy task for the amount of travelling they did. She cared for the people God entrusted to their care and she believed her diligence would one day grant her the great reward: to bear Abraham a son fulfilling his appointment by God to be the Father of all nations.

Sarah was chosen as each of us is chosen for a special Kingdom purpose.

Death – in the Desert

Sarah's lack of trust and mistreatment of Hagar were surely the death in her earthly story. Those decisions and events had to leave her feeling very unsettled and disappointed in her behaviors. She may have spent many nights pondering her lack of trust before the Lord and seeking repentance.

It is only by turning to God in humility, seeking His forgiveness and surrendering to His will for her life that Sarah will ultimately be redeemed.

Resurrection – birth of Isaac

The moment has come for Sarah to fulfill God's purpose for her life. In Genesis, chapter 21, we read,

> *"Now the Lord was **gracious** to Sarah as he had said, and the Lord did for Sarah what he had promised. Sarah became pregnant and bore a son to Abraham in his old age, at the very time God had promised him."*
> (Emphasis added)

There is that beautiful word. The word that offers hope. The word that gives birth to a resurrected and redeemed life: grace.

Sarah made mistakes, but Sarah was *so* faithful! I wish Scripture would go into more detail about her faithfulness and her deep and abiding love for God. God marks the resurrection of this story not only with the birth of Isaac but also by changing the names of Sarai and Abram to Sarah and Abraham. This is certainly a foreshadowing to the numerous conversions that occur throughout the New Testament where Jesus renames and repurposes the lives of His followers. It is also a reminder that God has a special name chosen for you and chosen for me. Since before the beginning of time, He has known you by name, and that is His great love for you. A love like no other.

Faith

Sarah's story is important because it reminds us of the damage that can occur when we focus on the improbability of God's promise ever being fulfilled in our lives rather than focusing on His promises **in faith**. In God's perfect timing, we know all things will be made new. Our lives can be made perfect by getting into agreement with God and aligning our will with His will for our life. So, right now you may be asking:

"This all sounds great, but what does this really have to do with me, a 21ˢᵗ century gal? Some days it feels like my purpose is to get the wash done and put away. I am nothing special and God hasn't shown me any unique and divine plan. I am nothing like Sarah. I am not special like that."

Yes! Yes, you are! You are special and you were specially created by God for an important job here on earth! We may not be called to populate the earth, or be the mother to the nations of Israel, but each of us has a special purpose, and I believe I know what it is.

Testimony

I had just attended a special service at a local church. I was 23 years old and was dating a Jewish man named Jacob. Jake had come to church with me that day. I was driving the car, and as we were pulling off the church property, I heard a voice I had never heard before say, *"I have something very special planned for you."* This absolutely shook me, and I quickly jarred the car and pulled on to the shoulder saying **"WHAT?"** Jake looked at me and said, "What are you doing, I didn't say anything!" I replied, "Shhh! It's not you." With that, I heard the voice again, *"I have something very special planned for you."*

I sat there for a moment collecting myself. Jacob was very respectful of my Christian faith. His father was Jewish, and his mother was a Christian who chose to raise their family Jewish. I had no idea what just happened except I knew I had heard the voice of God. Jake believed I had too.

Throughout my life, as different events took place, I would ask God, "Is this what you meant? Is this the special thing you told me would happen?" When we were adopting our children, I asked. When we took responsibility for caring for my husband's mother, I asked. When my husband became ill and I was fortunate to begin a career with our local hospital which provided great care to my hubby, I asked. Each time, God's answer was the same, *"This is wonderful, but this is not what I meant."* And so, it continued for twenty-five years. Never quite sure or knowing what God's *"something special"* was for me.

Until 12/14/13. My prayer journal entry that day is titled "The Awakening" and it reads like this:

You told me long ago that You "have something very special planned for me." For years...my whole life, I wondered what you meant. With every good thing that happened in my life I asked, "is this what you are speaking of Lord?" You would reply, "This is wonderful and indeed special, but this is not it."

*Today – you revealed to me your secret. Hebrews 13:1-21 reveals the meaning of life which I have always sought. In a word, You told me that the special plan You spoke of was to "**enter into full communion with You.**" You then showed me how my whole life has pointed to this truth and You said, "**you were commissioned when hands were laid upon you and you felt My Holy Spirit within you.**"*

Thank you, Lord, for choosing <u>me</u>, for choosing all of us to do your holy work and be your holy children. I love you, Father.

This is God's desire for you too. You are called to a very special purpose and that is to enter into a relationship of full communion with Him. It is what He desired for Eve and Sarah, Hagar and you and me. There it was in Hebrews 13:1-21. God lays out the plan for our lives. I had never read that chapter and verse before that very morning on 12/14/13 and I believe it was God himself who pointed me to that Scripture verse. Our calling is clear:

- Keep on loving each other.
- Be hospitable to all, especially the stranger.
- Remember those under oppression and imprisoned.
- Honor your marriage and all marriages.
- Do not worship money or claim your worth by how much money you have.
- Pray for all leaders.
- Submit to the truth: the teachings of Jesus Christ only.
- Through the High Priest, the Church, we offer our sacrifice of praise and receive Jesus Christ.
- Submit to authority.
- Work with joy not burden.
- Pray, pray, pray

Thank you, God! I can do this…sister, we *all can do this* and in doing so, live out our purpose! God may call some of us to do mightier things than this for His kingdom but imagine what our world would look like if we would all make it our daily work to live out these principles. One person at a time, we could bring the Kingdom to others and bring peace to all nations.

It is no coincidence how Sarah and Abraham's life fulfilled the principles that we read of in Hebrews. By living these principles, we remain in constant communion with God and allow for Him to use us for higher purposes.

 Go Deeper…

What Does it All Mean?

How has God used the experiences of your life to bring you closer to Him? Have you remained in constant communion with Him through these circumstances?

What Scripture verse have you been pointed to as your life verse and your call for holy living?

What is on your heart at this very moment to share with God?

On your knees…

Father bless us all! Bless us and protect us as You did our sister Sarah. You maintained her purity so that she could fulfill Your holy purpose for her life. Help us to remember even when we fall, as Sarah did, we need but come to You in faith and You will redeem us. Jesus never denied anyone healing who came to Him in faith. We need but touch the hem of your garment, in faith, and You will redeem us. Thank You for being the God who sees, the God who saves, the God who forgives and the God who pours out redeeming grace that we may enter in full communion with You and the host of heavenly saints. We love and praise You!

In looking at the final chapter of Sarah's life, we see she fulfills the promise God placed on her to bear the child Isaac on whom God establishes His everlasting covenant for all descendants. What exactly is this covenant? That Abraham's descendants, through Isaac, would be innumerable and God will be their God for all of history pouring on them all spiritual and physical blessings.

As Abraham's spiritual descendants, God's promises are ours as well.

Isaac is born and the joy of the Lord must have filled the land. I cannot even imagine Sarah's humility and joy at the birth of her son. The angelic choirs must have been proclaiming and rejoicing loudly that day!!! What beauty! What promise! The earth was filled with hope once again.

What a circuitous route Sarah took to get to this place. She endured many hardships, both physical, emotional and spiritual.

I pray that Sarah's life was filled with joy and continued communion and personal relationship with God and her family and that her final years were happy, reflecting a life based on faith, obedience and love of God.

Sarah. Asked by God to do the impossible at an impossible age. Yet, *"with God, all things are possible."* (Matthew 19:26)

Life Sentence…

If you were to sum up Sarah's life in one sentence, what would it be?

Part III

Leah & Rachel

11

Sisters

Are you familiar with the story of the two sisters, Leah and Rachel? Let me introduce them to you directly from the words of Scripture in Genesis 29:1-30:

> *29 Then Jacob continued on his journey and came to the land of the eastern peoples. ² There he saw a well in the open country, with three flocks of sheep lying near it because the flocks were watered from that well. The stone over the mouth of the well was large. ³ When all the flocks were gathered there, the shepherds would roll the stone away from the well's mouth and water the sheep. Then they would return the stone to its place over the mouth of the well.*
>
> *⁴ Jacob asked the shepherds, "My brothers, where are you from?"*
>
> *"We're from Harran," they replied.*
>
> *⁵ He said to them, "Do you know Laban, Nahor's grandson?"*
>
> *"Yes, we know him," they answered.*

6 Then Jacob asked them, "Is he well?" "Yes, he is," they said, "and here comes his daughter Rachel with the sheep."

7 "Look," he said, "the sun is still high; it is not time for the flocks to be gathered. Water the sheep and take them back to pasture."

8 "We can't," they replied, "until all the flocks are gathered and the stone has been rolled away from the mouth of the well. Then we will water the sheep."

9 While he was still talking with them, Rachel came with her father's sheep, for she was a shepherd. 10 When Jacob saw Rachel daughter of his uncle Laban, and Laban's sheep, he went over and rolled the stone away from the mouth of the well and watered his uncle's sheep. 11 Then Jacob kissed Rachel and began to weep aloud. 12 He had told Rachel that he was a relative of her father and a son of Rebekah. So she ran and told her father.

13 As soon as Laban heard the news about Jacob, his sister's son, he hurried to meet him. He embraced him and kissed him and brought him to his home, and there Jacob told him all these things. 14 Then Laban said to him, "You are my own flesh and blood."

Jacob Marries Leah and Rachel

After Jacob had stayed with him for a whole month, 15 Laban said to him, "Just because you are a relative of mine, should you work for me for nothing? Tell me what your wages should be."

16 Now Laban had two daughters; the name of the older was Leah, and the name of the younger was Rachel. 17 Leah had weak eyes, but Rachel had a lovely figure and was beautiful. 18 Jacob was in love with Rachel and said, "I'll work for you seven years in return for your younger daughter Rachel."

19 Laban said, "It's better that I give her to you than to some other man. Stay here with me." 20 So Jacob served seven years to get Rachel, but they seemed like only a few days to him because of his love for her.

21 Then Jacob said to Laban, "Give me my wife. My time is completed, and I want to make love to her."

22 So Laban brought together all the people of the place and gave a feast. 23 But when evening came, he took his daughter Leah and brought her to Jacob, and Jacob made love to her. 24 And Laban gave his servant Zilpah to his daughter as her attendant.

25 When morning came, there was Leah! So Jacob said to Laban, "What is this you have done to me? I served you for Rachel, didn't I? Why have you deceived me?"

26 Laban replied, "It is not our custom here to give the younger daughter in marriage before the older one. 27 Finish this daughter's bridal week; then we will give you the younger one also, in return for another seven years of work."

28 And Jacob did so. He finished the week with Leah, and then Laban gave him his daughter Rachel to be his wife. 29 Laban gave his servant Bilhah to his daughter Rachel as her attendant. 30 Jacob made love to Rachel also, and his love for Rachel was greater than his love for Leah. And he worked for Laban another seven years.

• •

The first time my sister met me, she threw up. Yup. My beautiful new-born, bouncing baby-self came home from the hospital on her seventh birthday. What a present! She took one look at me and lost her cookies, or uh… birthday cake.

I never held it against her. We have always been close and years later we even worked together in our father's business. Every February I would travel to Las Vegas for a trade show that fell over Valentine's Day. On one such trip, I opened my suitcase to find a Valentine card from her. In it she wrote:

If I have never told you before, I'm sorry I threw up the first time I met you!

I immediately called her and with tears streaming down my face we laughed and laughed. Best. Valentine. Ever!

For many women, sister or sibling relationships are very complicated. I don't understand that. I am beyond blessed with a sister that I have always respected, loved and have held in my heart with such gratitude. She and I have often commented that at least since that first intro, we are very lucky to have never had ill feelings toward each other. We have never been jealous of each other. I truly believe that my sister is the most beautiful, kindest, smartest, most generous woman in the world. And she is. If you were to ask her, she would tell you that *I* am the most beautiful, kindest, smartest, most generous woman in the world. And she would believe that with all her heart. We have been blessed by each other and we have each been a blessing to each other. Similarly, I have always called my sister-in-law Linda, my sister, and friend.

We believe the reason for this is that through everything we have shared, God has been the center of our relationship. We rarely speak that praises for Him do not pour from our lips. The same can be said of my brother and in-laws. It is a great blessing to be part of a family so rich in love for God and surrounded by men and women of faith.

Sibling relationships like ours cannot be taken for granted. I have met many women who have a sister relationship that more so resembles that of Leah and Rachel. Siblings whose relationships have been fraught with competition and favoritism bestowed on them by parents or other family members.

As in any relationship, the involved parties are responsible for their outcome. This responsibility can be tough to swallow, particularly when one feels wronged or justified in their feelings. There are even cases where it may be best to simply "love from afar." Jesus himself told us in Matthew 10:14, *If anyone will not welcome you or listen to your words, leave that home or town and shake the dust off your feet.* Yes, for any relationship to work both parties must be willing to be welcoming and be willing to listen, forgive and love.

Willingness. A character trait that often eludes us when we are feeling hurt or have had our feelings injured. Some situations destroy the willingness that we desire to exemplify when living a Christian life and is instead replaced by stubbornness, bitterness and loneliness.

Life, sisters, and relationships can be complicated! Willingness can quickly be eroded by hurt feelings.

As we dig deeper into the writing around their relationships and story, you will see that Scripture doesn't specifically reveal what the rivalry between Leah and Rachel stems from, however I have a pretty good guess. I could tell you that I spent months and months of intense study, reading hundreds of sources in both ancient and modern texts to uncover the source of their rivalry, but I didn't need to. I have drawn the conclusion that the basis for Leah and Rachel's conflict resulted from…are you ready?

J E A L O U S Y!

What could this jealousy have stemmed from? Hmmm…I wonder. Let's start with appearances.

Oh, heavens! Please tell me that how a woman looks hasn't mattered since the beginning of time? Really? Really!

When Leah and Rachel are introduced to us in Genesis 29, we learn the following:

Rachel – She was beautiful in form (her figure) and had a lovely face.

Rachel's beauty was so overwhelming to Jacob that when he met her, he *kissed her and began to weep aloud.* Perhaps he wept because he was hot and tired, and he was so grateful that she would take him to shelter? Perhaps he wept because he had travelled such a great distance and now, he was finally united with his mother's brother's family? Perhaps. It was probably a combination of all these things and because she knocked his socks off and he couldn't believe his good fortune in finding this beauty to spend the rest of his life with!

Leah – She was older. She had weak eyes.

That's all folks. That's what we learn about Leah. She's old…I mean "older" and unattractive. The New Living Translation Bible writes this in chapter 29, verse 17, "*there was no sparkle in her eyes.*"

Well, it actually says:

"There was no sparkle in Leah's eyes, but Rachel had a beautiful figure and a lovely face."

Yes, Leah has a nice personality, but that Rachel – she's the beauty! Oy!

Why is it we put so much emphasis on looks? Are we that shallow as a people?

Could there have been a reason why there was no sparkle in Leah's eyes? Certainly the sparkle in her eyes was present when she was lovingly and perfectly created by God. Could her God-given sparkle have dimmed with each passing comment, each neglecting word and each passing year as she heard how beautiful her sister was without knowing her own worth? Yes. That is what I believe happened, because I see it happen in women and girls today. Women take their worth from the world. Women take their worth, their value, from the wrong things and like Leah risk having the sparkle dimmed from their eyes.

The words people use to describe us and the way we allow people to treat us all can affect how we view ourselves this side of heaven.

As I think about this, immediately several real-life examples come to mind. I'm going to take you through a few case studies right now.

Case Study 1

Her parents grew up in athletics. They marry and have three daughters. Two are athletic but the middle child is not. She is beautiful and very smart. Enrolled in all honor classes, just not athletic. Parents don't comment on her intelligence but on her lack of athletic ability. "Not being good at sports" is how this girl defines herself.

What I pray this girl knows:

I am me. God's holy and chosen creation. I am not who my parents were.

Case Study 2

A woman I work with was neglected and verbally abused growing up. Her parents had wanted a boy. She spent her entire life over-achieving in an effort to win their affection. She is very successful, yet even as she nears retirement she is destroyed if her colleagues act as if they do not like her. Her priority in life is to be liked and accepted and she tries to achieve this not by being who she is (which is an amazing, generous woman) but rather she identifies herself by what she does.

What I pray this woman knows:

I am me. God's holy and chosen creation. I am not what I do.

Case Study 3

A woman I have ministered with shared with me that she has terrible self-esteem issues since her divorce. She had been married to a very successful president and CEO of a large corporation. Her life revolved around being the president's wife. Country club dinners, events, more dinners and more events were the landscape of her life. When her husband left her for the secretary, her entire world came crashing down. She lost her identity.

What I pray this woman knows:

I am me. God's holy and chosen creation. I am not who I marry.

Testimony

In 7th grade, my friend told me that if I wasn't chubby the boys would like me. She said, and I quote, "the boys would all like you if you weren't so, you know…fat." At the time, my pre-pubescent body was at the most three pounds overweight. Her statement, however, formed how I viewed myself. Quite honestly, I have spent most of my life, regardless of my weight, believing I was "chubby." I continue to run 3-4 miles most days trying to not be "chubby."

What I pray I have come to know:

I am me. God's holy and chosen creation. I am not what others say I am.

I pray Leah could see herself with God's eyes for her. I pray **you** can see yourself as God sees you.

 ## Go Deeper…

Guard your Sparkle

Who do you know that is having the sparkle dim from their eyes because of the words or actions of someone else?

Your case study #1

Is there one thing that you have fought your whole life based on something you were told? Are you currently working to change a perception that you view as possibly dimming to your own sparkle?

Friend, it is so important that you guard your heart and in doing so, guard your sparkle. You want your life to be bright and shining with the light of Christ. It is how God created you!

I pray that our words are like a cloth shining the sparkle of others, not dimming them. I pray our words and actions bring others to salvation, not suffering. I pray we increase each other's holy flame, not extinguish it.

As we consider this, let us rest in words from Scripture. Words that tell us *who we are because we are who God says we are!* Read the following verses and make them personal. *God is speaking to YOU!*

Isaiah 43:6 - *Bring my sons from afar and my daughters from the ends of the earth- Everyone who is called by my name, whom I created for my glory, whom I formed and made.*

You were formed and made by the Creator of the Universe. You are called by name. You are created for glory!

Matthew 5:16 - *In the same way, let your light shine before others, so that they may see your good works and give glory to your Father who is in heaven.*

Your light is shining! You are made for good works and to bring glory to your heavenly Father!

Made for His glory. Made to be holy and blameless in His sight. Made to rest in His love. Made beautiful. Believe it. Write out your personal affirmation below. You are not who man says you are. You are who God says you are. You are beautiful, strong and courageous, sparkling and loved!

12

Deception

Lying lips are an abomination to the LORD, but those who act faithfully are his delight. (Proverbs 12:22)

In college, I used to pride myself on the fact I could get any boy to like me. Yes. I sure had a high opinion of myself.

If I decided I wanted him to like me, I made him my mission. I was all about the chase. Once he liked me though, I moved on to some other boy. I have never really analyzed why I behaved like that. Maybe it had something to do with that 7th grade comment. Maybe somewhere inside was a pre-teen screaming, "See, the boys DO like me!" Maybe it was fear of commitment. The chase was the easy part. Relationships? Not so easy.

Only now, when I look back on that time, do I see how deceitful I was being. How dare I play with another person's mind and heart?

In our story this week, Jacob got played. He was clear from day one that he was in love with Rachel and wanted to marry her. Jacob was destined for greatness and would have been a prize for any father to give his daughter in marriage. Yet, Laban plays Jacob. He puts a price on the union: seven years of hard labor. Jacob willingly takes the deal and for seven years waits for his beloved. He works diligently to increase the flocks and property of Laban. On the wedding day, Jacob, a little tipsy from love and perhaps a good bottle of wine, is deceived when in the dark of night Laban sends in Leah to sleep with Jacob, thus consummating the marriage.

Think this through with me. Imagine Leah's shame the next morning when Jacob wakes up nuzzling her lovingly only to shudder and carry on when he realizes *she is not Rachel!* In that moment, after feeling his acceptance, she felt his rejection, as well as feeling deceived, betrayed and lower than she ever had.

Laban's deceiving Jacob leads to Leah being deceived as well. What a cycle!

Write out below the Scripture passage of Genesis 29:25

"What have you done to me," Jacob **raged** *at Laban.* (emphasis added)

Rage. Not the best emotion to wake up to on day one of happily-ever-after.

We can ask ourselves at this point, "Why did Leah go along with it?" Was it because she was eldest and as such should be the first to marry? Was she embarrassed at what her father was making her do? Did she try to resist Laban when he suggested this charade? Or was she happy to step in and replace Rachel because she was craving affection and acceptance?

Even if we come to a consensus that this was all under Laban's direction, do you think this is how Leah interprets it? Do you think she is going to blame her father? No! She will blame herself.

"If only I was prettier…"

"If only I had been a better lover last night, he would not want to leave me."

"I'm so pathetic that my father has to trick him into marrying me."

"It's my fault. I should have been honest with him when I entered the tent last night."

"Perhaps he can still find a way to love me and forget about Rachel."

"I hate my sister."

Yet hope springs eternal. Yes, I believe that after the initial shock, Leah turns from heartache to hopeful. After all, she now has *seven whole days* to win his affection before he takes Rachel as the second wife. So, what does this remind you of? Are you Leah? Have you been betrayed? Heartbroken? Lonely? Or, are you Jacob? Were you tricked? Were you lulled into believing something was true that wasn't?

On your knees...

Seeing God in this

Where do you see God in your situation?

Do you believe God is using your situation for a greater purpose? If so, how?

If not, pray right now on your knees and ask God to reveal to you the bigger picture. The billboard. Ask Him to show you where you can begin to trust again, to love again. You can certainly begin by trusting and loving Him. He will never hurt your heart. He will never break your trust. He will never forsake or abandon you.

. . . .

Be strong and courageous. Do not be afraid or terrified because of them, for the Lord your God goes before you; he will never leave you nor forsake you. **(Deuteronomy 31:6)**

13

Choices

Jacob is in his 2nd seventh year contract with Laban. He is now married to Leah and Rachel. It appears Jacob maintains his responsibility to both households. Leah discovers her way to Jacob's heart, or so she thinks. Leah believes the way to Jacob's heart is not through his stomach but through creating a family.

God, seeing the emotional torture that Leah is experiencing in her loveless marriage, *opens her womb*. (Genesis 29:31) Leah is now pregnant and presents Jacob with his firstborn son, Reuben – meaning "sees my misery."

Now, Leah believes she has found the nectar of life and the secret to finally winning Jacob's heart. "Surely if I bore him another child, he will surely love me…" Four times, in chapter 29, the Lord opens her womb and she gives Jacob a child. This must have created even stickier feelings between Leah and Rachel. Leah must have felt like she finally had the upper hand. As we have studied before, bearing children was a very important role for women in ancient time.

Terrible to think we would ever use children to gain the upper hand in a situation, yet I am not naïve. This still happens today. In ancient time and in modern time, children are often the victims in love triangles.

There are a few important lessons as we consider the way this family created their lineage. This season of their life was filled with competition and jealousy. We also see where these young mothers believe their value and their love come from these human relationships.

Look up the following verses with me.

Genesis 29:32 Leah bore a child named Reuben meaning_____

The Lord has noticed my _____, *surely now my husband will love me.*

Misery = child = love

Genesis 29:33 She bore another child named Simeon meaning "one who hears."

The Lord heard that I am not _____, *so he gave me another Son.*

Son = VALUE to Jacob

Genesis 29:34 Yet again, she bore a child and named this boy Levi which is derived from the Hebrew for "attached."

Now at last my husband will become attached to me, because I have borne him three sons.

Her belief was: Sons = Attachment = Love

Do you see how Leah identifies herself because of this tension between her, Jacob and Rachel? She is in "misery." She is of no "value." She is "unattached."

But God. The God who saw Hagar in the desert and gave her hope, desired to capture Leah's heart and bring her His hope and promise.

If I could sit across a table from Leah, I would say, "Sweet woman, you have this all wrong! This has absolutely nothing to do with Rachel and Jacob. This is about *you and God and you and God alone.* God is showing favor on you because He believes you can be the right mother for these sons who will be the twelve sons of Israel. God is working with you to fulfill His Promise through you! You have a specific purpose and were designed for a specific calling: to create the nations." Oh, if I could have a few moments to encourage her.

So let me encourage you. If you are feeling misery, not valued and unattached or lonely, friend, *God sees you. I see you.* You are loved. You are very important to the Body of Christ and the Kingdom of God on earth. You are important to God the Father and Jesus, His only Son. See what happens next when Leah begins to turn her focus to God rather than man.

In **Genesis 29:35** Leah bears a child Judah, whose name means "praise."

What was the change? When she conceived the fourth time, she began to "praise the Lord."

This is the lesson: Once Leah *surrendered* unto the Lord, she stopped having the need to prove anything to anyone. She became complete. Fulfilled. Perhaps she finally accepted that she would never possess Jacob's heart the way Rachel did. Perhaps she was too exhausted from having four children under the age of four! (ok...just guessing on that!) Who knows! What we do know is that it appears *she stopped fighting the enemy of competition and jealousy.*

Oh, friend, we don't always have to fight for freedom. So often **we need only *surrender* to live in peace and freedom, regardless of the circumstances. That's the secret!**

Let's repeat that: *We need only surrender to live in peace and freedom, regardless of the circumstances.*

It is necessary to remember Who we surrender to: God, the Great I AM. Jacob, most likely, still favored Rachel. It didn't matter. *Leah lived in God's peace and freedom.*

Rachel may have still been perceived more beautiful than Leah to the human eye. It didn't matter. *Leah lived in God's peace and freedom.*

The circumstances may not have changed, but Leah changed. Leah surrendered unto God. Leah became grateful for what she had. Leah got busy with the task of fulfilling God's plan for her life. Leah no longer needed a man to give her value. **She had discovered the secret.**

Leah was Leah. God's holy and chosen creation.

Go Deeper...

That Crazy Thing

Have you ever allowed a relationship to let you act in a crazy way or do crazy things? (Let's all nod our heads together in a yes motion.)

Looking back, do you see God's hand in the situation? Have you been able to gain peace regardless of the circumstances?

Many women report they have loved the wrong man or trusted the wrong friend. Perhaps you have a good relationship that is simply surfacing in the wrong season of your life. In every relationship, we run the risk of being disappointed if we set up expectations. Like Leah, we can become bitterly disappointed and brokenhearted. Yet the **secret** to peace is the same for us as it was for Leah. **Surrender to God.** Give **Him** your heart. Take your worth from the Word that tells you how much you are loved. His Word that tells you:

- You are holy and chosen. (Colossians 3:12)
- You are more beautiful than the lilies of the field. (Matthew 6:28)
- He knew you and loved you before you were even formed in your mother's womb. (Jeremiah 1:5)
- He has counted every hair on your head – that is how intimately He knows you. (Matthew 10:30)
- He is the love of your life. (1 John 4:19)

Take a few moments to write out your love letter to God. Express how you feel. Open your heart to Him and pour out your worries, anger, bitter frustrations and fears. Let Him wipe away your tears if they come. He will gently take your hand and lead you out of the dark waters that you feel yourself drowning in. He will walk beside you as you enter a new world where you realize you are worthy of His blessing because you believe in Him and love Him. Pour your heart to Him now and start over, as Leah did, with love in your heart and praise on your lips!

And Rachel was still barren....

Genesis chapters 30 and 31 describe what I like to call the "Baby Bowl." Rachel may have been beautiful, but beauty couldn't keep her from being desperate. Suddenly, it felt as though she had won the battle, but lost the war. *"How could my ugly duckling sister be fertile, and I am barren? This isn't supposed to happen this way. I'm the favorite. Everything good should happen for ME!"*

Spoiled. Spoiled. Spoiled.

Do you have a Rachel in your life? Have you ever acted like the Rachel we meet in these chapters? Oh, I have! I have been Leah and I have been Rachel. Most of us behave like this until we know the secret. Without the secret, we are lost. We compare ourselves to others. Our life is full of wanting and striving and sometimes that leads to conniving and making decisions that can ultimately have terrible consequences.

Do you know the secret? The secret is to **surrender** to God. We need to surrender to Him so His will for our life becomes our will. Paul speaks about this in many of his letters to the early church.

> *Do not be conformed to this world, but be transformed by the renewal of your mind, that by testing you may discern what is the will of God, what is good and acceptable and perfect.* (Romans 12:2)

> *Set your minds on things that are above, not on things that are on earth.* (Colossians 3:2)

> *Who can know the LORD's thoughts? Who knows enough to teach him?" But we understand these things, for we have the mind of Christ.* (1 Corinthians 2:16)

Thank God for His unconditional love and mercy that flow so freely and cover our sins and inequities!

Rachel's decision to have children through her servant reminds us of Sarah's use of Hagar. Rachel begins her family by using her servant. Let's look at chapter 30 and consider the names Rachel chooses for her children. To recap the preceding verses in chapter 29, by this time, Leah has had four children:

- Reuben, who was born because the Lord saw her misery

- Simeon, because the Lord heard she was not loved

- Levi, so her husband could be attached to her

- Judah, so she might praise the Lord

Let's look at what happens when Team Rachel enters the Baby Bowl.

Genesis 30:6

Rachel names her son Dan meaning_____

Genesis 30:8

Rachel names her child Naphtali meaning _____

Baby Bowl score: Leah 4 – Rachel 2

Then Leah gets back in the action again and the Baby Bowl begins! Since Leah's womb has apparently closed, Leah offers her maidservant to Jacob also.

Genesis 30:11

Leah names her child Gad meaning_____

Genesis 30:13

Leah names her child Asher meaning_____

Baby Bowl score: Leah 6 – Rachel 2

It's not over…now Leah begins to pay for the pleasure of her husband.

Genesis 30:16

Leah bears a child Issachar meaning_____

Then, Zebulon meaning_____

Baby Bowl score: Leah 8 – Rachel 2

God finally opens Rachel's womb and she bears Jacob a beautiful son named Joseph, meaning **"May he add."**

Joseph brings Rachel's number of male children to 3. She will have one more son named Benjamin which takes the score to Leah 8 – Rachel 4. In the end, Leah wins – but together, with their maid servants, they mother the twelve tribes of Israel.

All sons, until Leah births Dinah. So, what is the point? God can take our messes and make a beautiful message out of them. For all their bickering and fighting, these sisters are still credited as the mothers of many nations. We are concerned about Rachel though. What we see in her is a woman who doesn't quite seem to grasp or accept God as the supreme authority over her life as Leah does. In fact, when Jacob's families finally flee Laban's household, it is Rachel who steals her father's idols. This indicates to us the character of Rachel. She is willing to steal that which her father holds sacred. It also tells us that she herself is pagan. In chapter 31, we see how easily Rachel steals and lies. We see in her a woman who is never quite able to rise about her self-interest and find joy in loving others or gratitude for the bounty of blessings she has. Her life continues to be defined by the competition, yet God takes her character and continues to develop her and refine her.

Ladies, we each hold the same amount of space in our Father's heart. We each have His *entire* heart! Good, bad and indifferent – we are the same in His eyes. When you understand this, it certainly levels the playing field and makes competition absurd.

So, perhaps Leah wins the baby bowl and Rachel wins Jacob's affection, but life is short and time is precious.

In Genesis 35:16, we learn that Rachel dies during the birth of her son Benjamin, the twelfth son of Jacob. Irony.

That which she insisted on, eventually killed her.

I hope in those final moments, Leah was at her side assisting. I pray in those final moments the sisters reconciled. I pray Leah assured Rachel that she would watch over her children and I believe in those final moments, Rachel saw and received God.

Perhaps it was in those final moments and seeing the maturity with which Leah conducted herself, that even Jacob began to see her in new eyes. We know it is only Leah whose name is written to come from Jacob's lips nearing the end of his own life. In Genesis 49:29-31, Jacob asks his sons to bury him in the cave where Abraham, Sarah, Isaac and Rebekah rest and he says, "and there I buried Leah." In death, Leah receives the respect and honor from Jacob that she craved in life.

Rachel *died* by that which she *wanted*.

Leah *receives* what she wanted in *death*.

14

Leadership

"Winning is habit. Unfortunately, so is losing." Vince Lombardi

Leah and Rachel's leadership style is grounded in one simple truth: they want to win. At any cost, by whatever it takes: losing is not an option.

In reality, both sisters can claim victory:

Leah has more children.

Rachel has Jacob's affection.

It is with this mindset they raise their families. They raise their boys, the future twelve tribes of Israel, to win. These women are willing to count the costs on their path to victory. They were willing to:

- Have a broken relationship with their husband
- Have a broken relationship with each other
- Not process pain. With an eye on the kids and an eye on the finish line, they keep moving forward

This can be a typical behavior for the spiritually immature. God is sometimes approached as Santa Claus filling the wish list of their life. They don't see their role in fulfilling God's purpose. They can be resistant to coming into agreement with God. The sisters act as if they believe that they, not God, have ultimate control. What we often forget is it is **only with God that there is any control. We agree with Him and He works through us.**

The sisters suffer a bit from the early "Sarah Syndrome" taking matters into their own hands yet still praising God when it works out the way they wanted. This is a common behavior among the faithful. We believe in God, His promises and His ultimate goodness, but we don't live out this belief to our fullest ability. The sisters, like Sarah, take matters into their own hands and then give God a glancing moment of praise when it works out exactly how they desired. This is a slippery slope for it can lead to several outcomes.

- Things work out as we hoped or beyond our expectation and we praise God.
- Things work out as we hoped or beyond our expectation and we praise ourselves.
- Things don't work out and we blame God.
- Things don't work out and we blame ourselves.

I wonder if in the quiet moments the sisters recognized their sinfulness, their part in all of the drama of their life and sought quiet and sincere reconciliation with God. I ponder what would have happened if God hadn't provided for them? Would a song of praise still have poured from their lips?

Will it still pour from yours?

Do the sisters take any responsibility for the future fate of Joseph? Genesis 37:12-36 tells us the brothers attempt to kill Joseph, but instead sell him as a slave. Why? Because they were jealous of him. They were competitive toward each other and it appeared that Joseph was winning. Does this behavior surprise us when we consider how their mothers may have treated each other?

Perhaps Leah and Rachel had reason to bicker. They had a man, their husband, wedged between them. It all started with *their father* Laban, another man who was wedged between them and for whose affection they most likely competed. We know Laban, first, models this bad, dishonest and destructive behavior. His daughters behave in the same or worse fashion, and then their sons do the same. The behavior deteriorates with each generation, ultimately desiring **death** for a brother.

But God.

God ultimately brings peace, prosperity and victory to this family through Joseph, the sold and forgotten son. This beautiful story is summed up so perfectly in Genesis 50:20 with the verse, *"You intended to harm me, but God intended it for good..."*

As we consider leadership styles, we can see where this type of "winning" mentality can break down a unit, a team, a department, and yes, a family. If this type of mentality is what is driving our relationships, there will always be friction. *No one can win all the time.*

Leah may have won the baby bowl, but Rachel won the heart of Jacob. Which would Leah rather have had? The heart of Jacob. Which would Rachel rather have had? The children.

With a victory mentality, no one ever really gets exactly what they want because to "win" at all costs means exactly that: there are going to be great costs.

Just as there are winners and losers, there are also gains and losses. Leaders must decide what they are willing to lose, in order to gain. This will singularly depend on their motivation.

Leah and Rachel were in a sticky situation because what motivated them was jealousy. This, at the root of any decision, is going to have negative effects. Leaders must constantly ask themselves, "why" and "what."

- *"Why am I thinking this way?"*
- *"What is at the heart of this conflict/decision/desire?"*
- *"What is my motivation to make this decision/change/policy?"*

What motivates a leader is of utmost importance. What's interesting in our study so far, is both Sarah and the sisters took matters of birthright into their own hands. Yet, their motivation was different. Sarah was truly motivated by God's promise to her and Abraham. The sisters were motivated by jealousy, betrayal, deception, a desire to win by having the other lose. Same basic outcome yet, I believe, totally different motivation.

Notice I didn't say justification. I'm guessing if the sisters were like women I know there was a great deal of justification happening! We can hear it in the Scripture verses. They were justifying God's actions based on their own knowledge and feelings. Well, one thing we know about God is that His economy and reasoning rarely resemble our own. **Nothing is too big, too much or too hard for God.** Yet through the sisters' story, God makes a beautiful message from the mess. Through Leah and Rachel, God creates the twelve tribes of Israel by which His only begotten Son will be born.

Being motivated to win can be a very positive thing. Creative solutions are often born from a drive to improve and succeed. When plan A in life doesn't work, we want to have a plan B, or C…or Z. We want to keep going and not give up.

Yet, I caution you to keep God in the center of your plans. Look for His amazing hand at work in your life. Recognize that sometimes rejection is His protection in your life. *We need not win every battle to win the war!*

There is a whole lot of gray between the starting gun of the race and the finish line. The race is where we are tested, pruned and refined like gold in fire. I fully believe Leah and Rachel reached spiritual and emotional maturity. I believe Jacob came to love both women fully. Like every marriage, the way we finish looks much different than how we start on the wedding day. God gives us the days we need to accomplish what He has planned for us. He gives us the time we need to become refined and mature. Winning is amazing, yet the full measure of God is experienced in the journey, not at the finish line.

Go Deeper...

Pray

In considering the most pressing situation and/or decision you are currently facing, prayerfully and honestly consider how you might answer the following questions:

- *"Why do I desire this outcome?"*
- *"What is at the heart of this conflict/decision/desire?"*
- *"What is my motivation to make this decision/change/policy?"*

Write out your thoughts, in prayer, to God. Bring it to Him. Call a meeting with just the two of you with your goal of coming into agreement with God's plan for your life.

15

Redeemed

Humble yourselves, therefore, under the mighty hand of God so that at the proper time he may exalt you, casting all your anxieties on him, because he cares for you. 1Peter 5:6-7

Earlier this week, we talked about the secret. The secret of surrendering unto the Lord so we may receive His peace and grace, regardless of our circumstances.

Many of us don't get the one thing we want more than anything in our personal lives. We may dream of a husband's love, the corner office job, the respect of the PTA moms or the affection of parents. Perhaps, like Leah and Rachel, we desire children.

One of the greatest challenges in our lives is to accept the compensation God gives through Christ is to live in faith without envy but with a heart full of gratitude which leads to praise.

We all have that one thing we wish was different about our lives. Getting to the place where we can see God's hand in our circumstances is the prize! The only way to get to that prize is to surrender the circumstance unto the Lord. Whether your circumstance is a person or a situation, give it to God and **don't take it back!**

I first learned this from a dear woman named Pat. We were in a small group environment discussing this topic. Pat shared with us her son had become addicted to drugs and alcohol and one day, he walked out of the house and they could not find him anywhere. He had a credit card and Pat would try to track his whereabouts by the usage of the card. She lived on the East Coast and would fly to whatever region they had tracked the card being used. She was desperate to find and save her son.

On one such trip, they had a hot lead with an address. They were certain they would find him! When they got to the apartment and knocked on the door a very tough-looking man who was not their son answered. The exchange was not one of fairytales. Her son was not there nor had he been. This man had stolen her son's credit card.

She went home defeated and grieving her prodigal son. In a moment of clarity, she surrendered her son unto the Lord. She prayed, "Lord, I cannot help or protect him, but you can. In this moment, I completely surrender him unto You."

I sat there in awe as she told this story for I had a huge circumstance in my life I had been unwilling to surrender unto the Lord completely. My husband had been sick for so long. So many symptoms and no diagnosis. I was constantly surrendering his situation and then taking it back. So, I asked Pat, "what did you do when you surrendered it and took it back again?" She looked at me and her head tilted and she said, "I didn't take it back. That was it."

WOW! That was a radically new concept for me for I was on a see-saw of surrendering and then taking it back. Surrendering and then taking it back.

So, I tried it Pat's way. It took discipline to truly leave the burden and circumstance at the foot of the cross of Jesus, but it is possible with faith, in prayer.

Two years after Pat surrendered her son to the Lord, her own doorbell rang one night, and there he was. Her prodigal son returned home, ready and willing to receive the love and help he knew only his parents could provide.

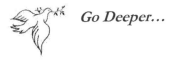 *Go Deeper...*

Surrender

What person, place or thing do you need to surrender unto the Lord?

What Bible verses can be a source of hope to you as you make the decision to turn this person or situation over to God? Remember, a great resource for this is www.openbible.info and type in keyword search, "surrender."

A verse that became significant in my ability to "let go and let God" is Hebrews 4:16:

> *16Let us then approach the throne of grace with confidence, so that we may receive mercy and find grace to help us in our time of need.*

One morning during my prayer time, God literally laid Hebrews 4:16 on my heart. I could hear him speak the words, "Hebrews 4:16." I picked up my Bible not even knowing there was a book in it called Hebrews. I assumed it had to be in the Old Testament since it was called Hebrews. It's not. It's in the New Testament. After I finally found it, I read the above verse. *God was speaking to me! He was showing me the secret!!* I literally dropped to my knees in tears and prayed in thanksgiving for His generous love.

This verse has become my battle cry when the weight of circumstances bears heavy. I know that all I need to do is "approach the throne of grace with **confidence**" and that God will hear and receive my prayer. It is all

God. His mercy. His grace. His unconditional, everlasting love.

No matter what is happening in your life, God is your constant source of strength, truth, mercy and love. These sisters created a lot of chaos in their lives, yet in the end, God's grace and mercy covered it all. That is the amazing way He works: His grace is sufficient. He is powerful in our weakness.

In 2 Corinthians 12:9, Paul reminds us of this truth when he writes, *But he said to me, "My grace is sufficient for you, for my power is made perfect in weakness." Therefore I will boast all the more gladly about my weaknesses, so that Christ's power may rest on me.*

Oh friend! The One who calls you is faithful. He is not going to bring you to a trial or temptation that He cannot bring you through! God did not put seeds of jealousy in the hearts of Leah and Rachel. He did not sow the seeds of competition. No, there was an enemy who was stoking those fires. God, though, in His great love redeemed these women by their children. He redeemed them through their marriage. He redeemed them as they sought Him.

Just my humble opinion but it feels as though a relationship with God came easier to Leah. That's often how it works. The one who is rejected by man often finds their way to God's protection sooner rather than later. Is there any relationship between hardship and rejection and finding your way to God? Is it easier or more difficult for those who are put on a pedestal in this world for their accomplishment, beauty or wealth to surrender their lives to the Almighty?

But God. He is patient. Faithful. He pours grace upon us to cover up the rough edges and soften our hearts toward Him and others. Your good, good Father did this for Leah and Rachel and He will do it for you.

~ If He brings you to it…He will bring you through it!

Go Deeper…

Change

Where are the rough edges in your life? Where are you hoping for God to make a lasting change?

God has done an amazing work in my life. I do not resemble the woman I was ten years ago. There have been financial struggles, health crises, depression, job changes, unemployment, raising kids, caring for aging parents, burying parents, home remodeling, and the recent placement of my fifty-nine-year old spouse in a nursing home. If you name something a marriage can go through, we have probably been through it. All of it in rapid succession. Things were bad, and then they got worse.

When things were bad, I went to God broken. Lost. Afraid. He showed me the weight of the cross where the battle is won. My job was to pick up the cross and in faith trust He would be my Simon carrying the weight with me.

In the end, we dealt with all those things I listed above…and more. I managed finances and health issues. We raised two amazing children. We fight the depression. I kept the job and even got promoted. None of it matters much though.

- What matters is the change that happened while face down in prayer on that rug in the prayer room.
- What matters is the tattered Bible that is highlighted, its margins filled with holy revelations.
- What matters is the love that bound us all together during the best and worst times.

- What matters is His grace. Flowing freely like water quenching a desert thirst.

He matters! God matters! And you matter to Him!

Yes, you do! So did Leah...and Rachel. It is why He makes miracles from our messes and He walks through the valley with us. No matter what your choices, He is waiting for you to come back. Leah and Rachel made some bad decisions – He loved them anyway. He loves you and He loves me. Even when we make bad choices too. He loves us. We are the same in His eyes. Holy. Chosen. Loved. Forgiven.

Father, we ask that we learn from Leah and Rachel to not look with envy on another woman. Each woman has her own worries, fears and heartache that she carries like a bag of rocks. Help us to grow in knowledge of Your Word so that we are armed with Your will for our life. Help us to lay down our bag of rocks at the foot of Your cross, thus creating an altar by which we can worship You, rather than holding on to the weight of our worry. Today, God, we give it all to You. We praise You and thank You for Your mercy and grace. Amen

Life Sentence...

If you were to sum up Leah & Rachel's life in one sentence, it would be?

Part IV

Ruth

16

Faithful Companion

*Don't urge me to leave you or to turn back from you. Where you go
I will go, and where you stay I will stay. Your people will be my
people and your God my God.* Ruth 1:16

The Hebrew meaning of the name Ruth is "female companion." How
fitting a name for one who travelled so honorably alongside another woman
as daughter and friend.

Ruth has the distinct honor of being the first female book in the Bible.
Ruth warrants our attention because her story teaches us to not accept
rejection as our fate in life. Ruth had many reasons to consider herself a
victim, yet by her trust in the God of Israel she becomes victor and is
delivered from the throes of her family legacy.

You see, Ruth was a Moabite. The Moabites were a thorn to the people of
Israel. You may recall from the Old Testament, Moab was born of the
incestuous act between his grandfather (Lot) and his mother (Lot's eldest
daughter). For the whole story, read Genesis 19:30-38. It's the stuff soap

operas are made of!

Moab's descendants had worshipped the god of Balaam and prayed for a curse to overcome the Israelites while they were camped out in Moab during the journey from Egypt into the Promised Land. The Israelites were seduced into worshiping the gods of the Moabites and over 24,000 Israelites died by plague in judgment over worship of this false god. (For that whole story, read Numbers 25:1-9) As if this wasn't bad enough, when the Israelites settled in Canaan, the Moabites attacked them there as well. To say that the Israelites' hatred of the Moabites ran deep is an understatement. Quite a soap opera, isn't it?

The decision for Ruth to marry an Israelite speaks volumes to her character and we can probably say, her faith. Ruth and Orpah are the daughters-in-law to Naomi and Elimelech. By some odd occurrence, all three of the women's husbands die. The Bible doesn't tell us how, although it is very odd that the three women should all be widowed around the same time.

As we learned in our study of the ancients in week two, to be widowed meant to have no rights. Widows were left to fend for themselves. They had to find their own food and shelter. They had no protection, no rights. In Moab, there were no real prospects for these women to marry but Naomi had a very good network back in Bethlehem, and so she and the girls decide to head back to Naomi's hometown.

Let's sit down together a moment and read the story of what happens when Naomi loses her husband and sons as recorded in Ruth, chapter 1.

> *1 In the days when the judges ruled, there was a famine in the land. So a man from Bethlehem in Judah, together with his wife and two sons, went to live for a while in the country of Moab. 2 The man's name was Elimelech, his wife's name was Naomi, and the names of his two sons were Mahlon and Kilion. They were Ephrathites from Bethlehem, Judah. And they went to Moab and lived there.*
>
> *3 Now Elimelek, Naomi's husband, died, and she was left with her two sons. 4 They married Moabite women, one named Orpah and the other Ruth. After they had lived there about ten years, 5 both Mahlon and Kilion also died, and Naomi was left without her two sons and her husband.*

Naomi and Ruth Return to Bethlehem

⁶ When Naomi heard in Moab that the LORD had come to the aid of his people by providing food for them, she and her daughters-in-law prepared to return home from there. ⁷ With her two daughters-in-law she left the place where she had been living and set out on the road that would take them back to the land of Judah.

⁸ Then Naomi said to her two daughters-in-law, "Go back, each of you, to your mother's home. May the LORD show you kindness, as you have shown kindness to your dead husbands and to me. ⁹ May the LORD grant that each of you will find rest in the home of another husband."

Then she kissed them goodbye and they wept aloud ¹⁰ and said to her, "We will go back with you to your people."

¹¹ But Naomi said, "Return home, my daughters. Why would you come with me? Am I going to have any more sons, who could become your husbands? ¹² Return home, my daughters; I am too old to have another husband. Even if I thought there was still hope for me—even if I had a husband tonight and then gave birth to sons— ¹³ would you wait until they grew up? Would you remain unmarried for them? No, my daughters. It is more bitter for me than for you, because the LORD's hand has turned against me!"

¹⁴ At this they wept aloud again. Then Orpah kissed her mother-in-law goodbye, but Ruth clung to her.

¹⁵ "Look," said Naomi, "your sister-in-law is going back to her people and her gods. Go back with her."

¹⁶ But Ruth replied, "Don't urge me to leave you or to turn back from you. Where you go I will go, and where you stay I will stay. Your people will be my people and your God my God. ¹⁷ Where you die I will die, and there I will be buried. May the LORD deal with me, be it ever so severely, if even death separates you and me." ¹⁸ When Naomi realized that Ruth was determined to go with her, she stopped urging her.

¹⁹ So the two women went on until they came to Bethlehem.

Imagine for a moment what their life was like before the loss of their husbands. I picture happy days of working together in the garden and in the kitchen. Naomi teaching the young women how to prepare the family favorites. The young wives caring for Naomi as their own mother while she grieved the loss of her husband and became the matriarch and leader of the family. The young men strong and capable. Their days were most likely filled with security. Stability. Love. Family.

Then disaster strikes and both sons die. Now three widows turn to each other for comfort and attempt to figure out how to take care of themselves.

We have mentioned this before, but widows had very few rights in the ancient world. The loss of a husband in ancient Israel was a social and economic tragedy. The widow was immediately marginalized and considered to be living in poverty. Disillusionment and bitterness could easily erupt in the woman's heart and we see this in Naomi. It reminds us how quickly life can change. Five minutes before, the women had everything and five minutes later, they have nothing.

Concerned with how they would survive, Naomi decides to return to Bethlehem where she has heard of the Lord's provision for His people. This hope brings them the courage they need to set out on their journey.

However, along the road to her hometown, Naomi realizes the need for the girls to return to their own homeland and begin over. They were most likely young enough to marry again. She releases them and gives them permission to return to their home, their people, their gods, and begin a new life.

Orpah takes the permission and leaves. Ruth stays. Both decisions took a mountain of courage.

Scripture tells us they wept loudly again at the thought of separating. I imagine their grief was the result of so many things: broken dreams, the what-ifs, fear of the journey that they were on. Would they even reach their destination alive? These were very real concerns.

Naomi nearly begs Ruth to return with Orpah, but Ruth refuses. Faithfully, she is determined to remain with Naomi. This is her family now. These are her people and most certainly, Naomi's God is now her God.

Scholars believe that Ruth remained with Naomi for more reasons than family loyalty: Ruth was also in love with Naomi's God. This love prevented her from returning to the land of the Moabites and their practice of worshiping false gods. She now knew the love of the Almighty and powerful Creator. She knew the stories of the Israelites' triumph over the Egyptians and their travels through the wilderness. She knew of God's might and his victory and, most of all, His love. Ruth wanted to worship this one, true God! She was in love with *our* God! The One *we know* and love and worship. When we follow God, crazy things can happen. We make decisions that seem insensible to the rest of the world. Naomi realized this and stopped urging her to leave. Together, the women travel on until they arrive in Bethlehem.

Bethlehem. The tiny town that is going to have a big future.

Bethlehem. Where hundreds of years later, a star guides the highest kings and the most lowly shepherds toward a humble stable to meet the Savior.

Wonderful things happen in Bethlehem.

17

Kinsman-Redeemer

"There is a time for extravagant gestures. There is a time to pour out your affections on one you love. And when the time comes – seize it, don't miss it." Max Lucado

Ruth and Naomi have very real needs once they arrive in Bethlehem. Yes, they have survived the trip and surely many emotional and physical hardships along the way. Two women traveling alone could not have been safe. Now they are at their destination. The whole town is stirring with gossip at Naomi's return. Naomi may as well be wearing sackcloth and ashes for her grief is apparent to all. Let me provide a summary to set the stage for you based on the book of Ruth, chapter 2. *(Do not miss the beauty of this love story. Please read the entire book of Ruth. It will take you approximately 20 minutes – don't miss out!)*

Naomi recalls a relative on her husband's side who was a "man of good standing" named Boaz.

As the women arrive in Bethlehem the barley harvesting is about to commence.

Ruth requests to go to the fields of Boaz and gather the barley that has been left behind by the harvesters.

It isn't long before Boaz sees the young woman in his field and asks his foreman who she is.

The foreman explains that she is a Moabite who has returned to Bethlehem with Naomi. Boaz in his kindness brings Ruth under his care instructing her to assist his servant girls. He assures her that the men have been instructed "not to touch you." Ruth is overwhelmed by his generous kindness and bowing before him asks, *"Why have I found such favor in your eyes that you notice me – a foreigner?"* Boaz replies, *"I've been told all about what you have done for your mother-in-law since the death of your husband...May the Lord repay you for what you have done."*

Sisters, are you swooning? Is this not the makings of a GREAT love story? Sigh...swoon...sigh again...

This story is so much bigger than a beginning love story between Boaz and Ruth. The book of Ruth is a love story between God and woman. Ruth's story so clearly shows us what we have been discussing throughout this book and the study of our other leading ladies. God's love for you has been since before the beginning of time. Let's consider this love as we look at some of the most beautiful names given to God, in both the Hebrew and the English.

- He is God, Mighty Creator, *Elohim*
  - o Creating beyond the heavens and earth, but also creating opportunities and relationships
- He is the God who sees, *El Roi*

He sees what you are going through. He sees you amidst your circumstances and He sees you with eyes that know the plans and purpose of your future. He saw Naomi and Ruth along the road traveling to Bethlehem. He counted every tear they shed upon the loss of their men. He felt the hunger pangs within their stomachs. He provided them rest and energy to make the long trip. He was their courage and their strength for the journey. He saw them and He sees you on your journey!

- He is the God who heals, *Yahweh Rapha*

o Healing hearts, healing minds and healing lives. He will do this for Ruth and Naomi and He will do it for you. Pause for a moment and consider the stories of our leading ladies, all healed through His love and grace.

- He is the God who provides, *Jehovah-Jireh*
  o Providing for Ruth and Naomi's physical needs (food, shelter) as well as providing a future for them through their Kinsman-Redeemer.

In this short book of the Bible, a short story really, we see God's hand moving so swiftly and so purposefully to return their broken lives to holy order.

Go Deeper...

God and you

Each name, and the many titles of God are introduced throughout Scripture. Take a few moments to reflect on the names and titles shared below with their corresponding Bible verse, and consider how God has shown His promises true in your life:

Elohim – Creator

Introduced in Genesis 1, *Elohim* is the plural form of *El (God)*. Genesis begins with the verse, "In the beginning God created the heaven and the earth." We are introduced to the plural form of this word in Genesis 1:26, as it is written "Let us make man in **our** image and **our** likeness…"

Our God as Creator.

Reflect a moment on God's creation. Reflect on the physical beauty that you witness each day but go deeper and consider what God has created within you. What has been born in your character? What dreams have been born (created) in your life? Where does your heart lie right now with those dreams? Write down those areas of creation in your life and offer a prayer of thanksgiving for all that God has created in you, for you and through you.

El Roi – God who sees

Introduced in Genesis 16:13-14 when Hagar is at the lowest point in her life. She has literally wandered off to die. She was at the end. No hope. At that precise moment, the Angel of the Lord appears to her and speaks to her, offering her hope once again. This hope, however, is more than a feeling. This hope is a person. Many scholars believe the appearing of this Angel of the Lord is a Christophany – a glimpse at the pre-incarnate Christ. That would make sense, wouldn't it?

Have you ever cried out to the Lord when you couldn't take one more circumstance rising in your life? I sure have! I've cried. I've yelled. I've screamed out, "*Why don't you do anything? Don't you see this???*" Often at that moment, a text will ring out. A song will come on the radio. A thought will come to my mind and calm me. The Presence of God manifests in many ways. We don't all get to see the Angel of the Lord up close and personal, but each of us can experience God's presence every day.

Our God who sees.

Recall a time when you thought hope was lost and then you received your miracle. Offer a prayer of thanksgiving for all that God has seen and done in you, for you and through you.

Yahweh Rapha– God who heals

The first mention of God healing His people, is found in Exodus 15, verse 26:

*26 He said, "If you listen carefully to the LORD your God and do what is right in his eyes, if you pay attention to his commands and keep all his decrees, I will not bring on you any of the diseases I brought on the Egyptians, for **I am the LORD, who heals you**."*

Let's pause a moment here and assess the verse above. Notice that before *God will heal you* there is a command for what *we must do*. We are called to "*listen carefully to the Lord our God and do what is right in his eyes, pay attention to His commands and keep all His decrees,*" then *the Lord will heal you*.

Do I believe God in His mercy can heal anyone? Of course! But we must also have realistic understanding as to what is our part in this. In the above verse, we are called to:

- Listen carefully to the Lord our God
- Do what is right in His eyes
- Pay attention to His commands and keep His laws

Can God come in and absolutely grant favor and healing and abundant blessing to whomever He chooses? Sure! He is God. Yet, when we study God's Word, we see time and time again examples like the one above. Our relationship with Him is like any relationship. There is give and take. No relationship can flourish if each party is not making the other party a priority. God will bless us every time He sees us making the effort to come to Him in prayer, to speak to Him, to listen and to be obedient. Some blessings (healing) will be notable, others we may not see for many years. That is what I believe the verse above tells us. "Be obedient to me...trust me...and I will heal you." The key word in all of this is trust. Trusting God is where the battles and wars are won. It is why throughout this study I repeatedly invite you into a personal relationship with God and His beloved Son, Jesus Christ. You cannot trust someone you don't know. Oh, friend, I want you to know and trust Jesus as if He were sitting next to you right now. Because He is.

God loves to heal His people. Jesus' three years of public ministry are filled with stories of healing (the leper, the blind, the bleeding woman, the possessed man, the sick child and many, many more)

God desires the healing of our physical health, spiritual health and emotional health. It is why He left us His written Word, that we may gain a glimpse of His character and His desire for us. It is why He left us the Holy Spirit to assist in interpreting and guiding us.

Our God who heals.

Reflect a moment on something that may need healing in your life. Have you brought this brokenness before the Lord in prayer? Have you studied His Word to see what He says about your circumstance? Have you trusted Him to faithfully attend to you in His perfect timing? Write down your thoughts, right now at this moment. Pour your heart of sorrow onto this paper and offer a prayer of thanksgiving for all God has healed in you, for you and through you.

Jehovah-Jireh – God who provides

Introduced in Genesis 22, verse 14, after Abraham is spared offering his son Isaac as a sacrifice to the Lord. Scripture tells us, "*So Abraham called that place The Lord Will provide…*"

Often when we think of God providing for us we think of physical needs like food, shelter, money, clothing. Yet in this story from the Old Testament, we learn that God often provides something else: He can often a provide *a way out*.

For Abraham, the way out spared his son's life. For some, the way out may be a promotion they don't receive, a job they aren't chosen for, or a relationship that ends. The way out can look very different to many people. But God. He has a plan and purpose for your life and He will do what He needs to do to bless and protect you always.

Our God who provides.

Reflect a moment on when you felt the Hand of God providing for you or saving you from going down the wrong path. Offer a prayer of thanksgiving for all God has provided within you, for you and through you.

18

Blessings

When I started counting my blessings, my whole life turned around.
Willie Nelson

When we first read this story and consider the landscape of these women's lives, blessings may not be the first word that comes to mind. But God, ever faithful, is also a God of surprises. Their struggle is very real, yet amid the struggle, God shows up in nine separate blessings.

I love this part of Ruth's story. These blessings remind and teach us that the words we utter have power. Within each day, we have an opportunity to bless or curse the people we encounter. As we consider the rest of Ruth's story, let us study these nine blessings. In Scripture, the number nine symbolizes divine completeness or conveys the meaning of finality. As we study these blessings, we will see how God has used these blessings to complete His purpose for Ruth. If you have not yet read the entire book of Ruth, now is the time!

The first of these blessings, found in the Book of Ruth, is given by Naomi in chapter one, verses eight and nine:

"May the Lord show kindness to you, as you have shown to your dead and to me. May the Lord grant that each of you will find rest in the home of another husband."

As I read through the first chapter of Ruth, two things struck me:

1) Like Lot's wife, Orpah is too afraid to move forward to the unknown. Given the opportunity, she chooses to go back to her homeland. Her desire to remain in what is familiar is greater than her desire to step out in faith.

- When have I chosen to remain in a situation that was comfortable even though I had the opportunity to move forward in faith?
- When, like Ruth, have I stepped out of my comfort zone and walked forward in faith?

2) Ruth responds to Naomi in poetic verse that is now considered "Ruth's Song." These words, which have been made into the popular hymn "Wherever you Go," are very comforting to us on our faith journey and, ironically, are words to a hymn often sung at weddings. These words speak to Ruth's character and her loyal commitment to follow Naomi and the God of Israel.

Now open your Bible and read through Ruth chapters 2-4. Don't cheat yourself out of this beautiful story by moving ahead in this study. Take some time to close this book and pick up THE book and read the rest of the Book of Ruth.

The nine blessings proclaimed in the Book of Ruth remind us that the words we speak to each other have great power! Speaking a blessing unto another's life may be the greatest gift we can give them. Let us take this time to review these nine blessings and consider how our speech can positively impact another and perhaps, like in the book of Ruth, change the trajectory of their life. After each of the blessings outlined below, consider who in your life needs such a blessing prayed or spoken over them.

Blessing 1   **Ruth 1:8-9**

"May the Lord show kindness to you, as you have shown to your dead and to me. May the Lord grant that each of you will find rest in the home of another husband."

Naomi is willing to let go of her daughters-in-law. She is willing to sacrifice her needs for their future. Is there anyone or anything in my life I need to emotionally let go of? Who is grieving right at this moment that may need my prayers and blessing? Who are the people or the things that I need to release unto God?

Blessing 2   **Ruth 2:4**

"The Lord be with you! The Lord bless you!"

What a beautiful way for the boss, Boaz, to greet his workers. How do I greet those I encounter? Is my Spirit welcoming? Do I consider others' needs before my own? How can I bless someone today?

Blessing 3 and 4   **Ruth 2:12-13**

"May the Lord repay you for what you have done. May you be richly rewarded by the Lord, the God of Israel, under whose wings you have come to take refuge."

Ruth has an opportunity to repay Boaz's kindness not by giving him anything, but rather by blessing him and praying for his continued success.

Do I think I *deserve* the good things that happen to me, or do I seek to repay kindness with kindness and ask for God to multiply the good in someone else's life before considering my own? Who can I pray for today that God may multiply every good thing in their life and give them abundance?

Blessing 5   **Ruth 2:19**

"Blessed be the man who took notice of you!"

Naomi recognizes God's great hand in steering Ruth to Boaz's field. Naomi seeks a blessing for Boaz in thanksgiving for his great kindness to Ruth.

Do I rejoice in the kindness of another and seek God's continued blessing for them? Who can I pray for today and ask God's blessing upon them for their continued kindness toward me and the ones I love? (A teacher? A coach? A ministry leader? A friend's mom or dad? My supervisor? My spouse's supervisor?)

Blessing 6   **Ruth 2:20**

"The Lord bless him! He had not stopped showing his kindness to the living and the dead."

Naomi expresses her appreciation for Boaz, who she now describes as her family's kinsman-redeemer. Who are the people who have saved me? The neighbor who helped plow my snow? The friend who picked up my child from school? The person who dropped everything at a moment's notice to come to my aid? How can I pray a blessing for the helpers in my life?

Blessing 7   **Ruth 3:10**

"The Lord bless you my daughter."

Boaz is surprised by Ruth's presence at his feet. He speaks his willingness to be her kinsman-redeemer. Is there anyone in my life that is seeking my help? Are my eyes open to them or have I been ignoring their cries for help? Who can I bless today by my presence, provision and protection?

Blessing 8   **Ruth 4:11**

"May the Lord make the woman coming into your home like Rachel and Leah who together built up the family of Israel. May you have standing in Ephratah and be famous in Bethlehem. Through the offspring the Lord gives you by this woman, may your family be like that of Perez whom Tamar bore to Judah."

A prayer for families. A prayer for success. Little did the elders know they were speaking a true proclamation of the ages: Ruth and Boaz would be, in a sense, famous in Bethlehem. For their great-great-grandson would be

King David whose lineage would bring forth the King of Kings, a baby wrapped in swaddling clothes born in a Bethlehem manger. Do I pray a blessing for the ages over my loved ones? Do I pray for generation after generation to know the Lord intimately and to be blessed and saved by Him?

Blessing 9   **Ruth 4:14-15**

"Praise be to the Lord, who this day has not left you without a kinsman-redeemer. May he become famous throughout Israel. He will renew your life and sustain you in your old age."

The women now pray a blessing over Naomi. From her ashes came beauty in the form of a devoted daughter-in-law and kinsman redeemer. Naomi is wished well and the blessings of the Lord are asked for her. Do I wish the women in my life well? Do I keep jealousy out of my relationships and truly pray for their well-being and success?

What a story! From Naomi's sadness, came abundant blessings. Out of Ruth's faithfulness to her husband's family, comes fortune. Ruth and Naomi had the opportunity to live their lives as victims. Yet, instead of remaining resentful and bitter, Ruth chooses a path of obedience. She loves God and therefore follows His law. She remains faithful to God and faithful to her family on earth. She works hard to provide for her mother-in-law and by God's intervention, she happens on to the fields of Boaz.

Ruth's relationship with Boaz is divinely appointed. Yet, she doesn't rush into anything. She waits and in God's perfect timing, she is given to Boaz. Boaz, too, remains obedient to God's love and laws. These two do everything by the book. The result? Abundant blessing and favor of God. Ladies, Ruth is a woman by whom we can emulate everything she does:

- Loyalty to family
- Bravery
- Persevering and hard-working
- Lawful
- Provider
- Convert to one true faith (at that time – Judaism)
- Faithful to God
- Blessing to others for as Ruth is blessed, she is a blessing unto others, particularly Naomi.

When we look at Ruth's whole life, it seems to be picture-perfect and wrapped up with a neat little bow. It's easy to forget the hard stuff. The messy middle where she didn't know what would happen and she put her total reliance in God. Often when we are in the middle, it's hard to imagine things will ever work out. The fact is, in the middle of the mess, it's hard to believe a blessing is coming.

If you are feeling right now like you are doing everything right, but nothing is going your way, take heart! Press in and take it all to God in prayer. Dig way down into this study of Ruth and consider all the moments in between that aren't recorded. The moments she and Naomi were hungry and without food. Perhaps they were dreaming of a fish dinner when the Lord sent them wheat. It wasn't what they wanted, but it satisfied their needs.

Read between the lines and find your hope there. Just like Hagar, you and I sometimes feel unnoticed. But God. He is the One who sees. He saw Hagar in the desert. He saw Ruth and Naomi and He sees you.

Find comfort and courage in the story of Ruth. She is a woman we can learn from and model some of our behaviors after.

Which characteristics of Ruth do you have? Which characteristics would you like more of?

Father, thank you for the example of Ruth that we may follow and obey Your laws and remain within Your love, all the days of our lives!

19

Influencer

The key to successful leadership today is influence, not authority.
Ken Blanchard

Looking at Ruth's story through a lens of leadership, we can quickly classify Naomi as a female who exhibits tremendous leadership abilities. Even amidst her own grief, Naomi took charge.. She wanted a better life for herself and Ruth and she was willing to sacrifice everything, even her own life, to return to her home land. Once they arrived in Bethlehem, we see Naomi very strategically managing Ruth and the relationship with Boaz. Naomi is seen as a very mature leader in this story and a woman who exemplifies great courage and strategic thinking.

Yet, Ruth allows us to look at leadership from a different view. Ruth's leadership teaches us the importance and value of influence. Influence is defined as *"the capacity to have an effect on the character, development, or behavior of someone or something, or the effect itself."* By this definition, we can see Ruth wielded great influence over both Naomi and Boaz.

Naomi may have been the natural leader, but Ruth is a willing and committed follower.

Imagine the boost to Naomi's courage when Ruth insists on traveling with her to Bethlehem. Imagine Naomi's joy to know that beyond Ruth's love for her is her interest in knowing Naomi's God. As an older woman mentoring a younger woman, this would certainly get your attention and you would want to pour everything you had into such a woman. Influence. By her actions, Ruth has influenced Naomi to be her mentor.

Leadership: Both women have it. Both women share it and bless each other with it.

This idea of woman walking alongside woman, discipling and growing in faith and fellowship inspired the 2019 birth of the ministry *Women Gathered*. Founded with my dear friend and Christian author, Deborah Lovett, this online community is centered around one woman discipling, equipping and influencing another. It's a little bit like church on Facebook. The group engages in regular Bible study and a whole lot of prayer. One woman sharpening another. One woman influencing another. (Check us out! Find our group Women Gathered on Facebook and join us!)

Imagine the influence of Ruth on the other women working in the field, knowing she had the attention of Boaz. Imagine the influence she had on Boaz. This simple girl, willing to follow the instructions of her elder mother-in-law and do everything she is told. You see, the leader in Naomi saw the opportunity that was before them for Ruth to marry Boaz. Ruth may not have been fully aware of this but she remained committed to Naomi and trusted her by doing everything she was instructed to do.

In Ruth, we see two angles of leadership: commitment and influence. Ruth remains committed to Naomi, and later Boaz, and shows influence over both.

And God blesses this influence.

Ruth becomes the great-great grandmother to King David and is forever placed in the lineage of Jesus Christ.

Go Deeper...

Influence

We can surround ourselves with people who are both a good or bad influence on us. Today, I want you to consider the following questions. Look deep into your relationships and into your heart. This is your exercise. As human beings, it is easy to do a study like this and start answering these questions for other people. This exercise is not about who influences your partner or your children. This is all about YOU!

Who influences you? *Write out the names of the people who influence you and how they influence you.*

Who do you influence and how? *Write out the names of the people you influence and how.*

Do you have a mentor? What is their name? Do you meet regularly with this person?

What is one thing you have learned from your mentor? What is one thing you wish to still learn?

Do you mentor any women? If so who and how?

What is one special thing that has come out of this relationship? (something you learned, something you taught them, etc.)

Women were created to support others. It's in our DNA. We are the nurturers. It is so important for us to realize that like Naomi and Ruth, **we are co-workers and not competitors on this path of life.** We see in Leah and Rachel how destructive that female competition can become. It is toxic. To balance that, with Naomi and Ruth we have examples of this beautiful, collaborative and supportive relationship. Each woman trusting the other and working toward a common goal.

Write down the name of one woman in your life where you have a Naomi/Ruth relationship? If you can't think of one that you have now, is there a woman you would like to have this type of friendship with? Write her name down here.

Pray for all the women you have written down on these pages. Take their names directly to the throne room of the Father and in the name of Jesus by the power of the Holy Spirit, speak their names unto the Lord. Ask God to bless, heal, protect and provide for these women as He did for Ruth and Naomi.

20

Redeemed

Ruth's story is a true story of redemption. We see so clearly how her sorrow turns to dancing. Literally.

This is such a story of redemption that Boaz, himself, is referred to as her "Kinsman Redeemer."

Every time I read the Book of Ruth, I am reminded of my own Kinsman Redeemer, Jesus Christ. Just as God chose Ruth to have a special place in His Kingdom, He has made that same choice for you and that same choice for me. Crazy, unexplainable, over-the-top LOVE.

As we look at the lesson of Ruth, we really catch a glimpse of our own love story with Jesus Christ.

He is the One who came to redeem us: to heal, protect, provide and bless us.

We see in Ruth's story how redemption can pour onto us and overflow unto others, as it blesses Naomi in addition to Ruth herself.

Sister, we are almost through the Old Testament with only one more woman to study. This seems like the right place for me to check in with you and be sure that you are secure in knowing that Jesus Christ is your Redeemer. He came into this world to save YOU. It's not something He did only for the Bible-quoting, church-going folk. He came for ALL so that every one of us might be saved.

I grew up knowing the love of Christ, but it wasn't until life really spiraled out of control that I turned my life over to Him. People often wonder what they have to do to be saved. It's so simple.

Make the decision today, right now, to turn your life over to Christ and accept Him as your Savior and Redeemer. That's all.

Perhaps you have already done this and so let us use this day to re-commit to Jesus Christ, just as Ruth re-committed to Naomi on the road outside of Moab. Our God is the God of second chances and for making old things new.

Pray with me, right now. If possible, let's get on our knees together and pray:

Father, I know You have created me and chosen me for something special. Sometimes life doesn't feel like I am on a path to glory, but I know in my heart that You are speaking directly to me right now. On my knees I come humbly before You and proclaim that I believe You are God the Father and that You sent Your Son Jesus Christ to save me. Right now, I commit my life to Jesus Christ and believe that He is my personal Savior. He is my Redeemer. By His death and resurrection, I live. Father thank You for the gift of faith that allows me to come before You. I come before You broken but will rise up blessed. Thank You for the gift of Your Son, my Savior Jesus Christ. In His Name, I pray this, Amen.

Welcome to the Body of Christ. You are forever changed and made new.

 Life Sentence...

If you were to sum up Ruth's life in one sentence, what would it be?

Part V

Esther

21

Silent Yet Present

There comes a special moment in everyone's life, a moment for which that person was born. That special opportunity, when he seizes it, will fulfill his mission — a mission for which he is uniquely qualified. In that moment he finds greatness. It is his finest hour.
Winston Churchill

Her birth name was Hadassah meaning "myrtle" or "fragrance." We know her as Esther, a Hebrew name meaning "Star." We are smart to immediately pay attention to this woman, whom God chose for a special task.

Esther was, perhaps, the most beautiful woman in the world. Unlike some of our past heroines, though, Esther does not define herself in this way. She defines herself as a precious child of her family and a precious daughter of God. Esther has inner and outer beauty which tells us: she is a woman of substance and character.

Esther is a rags to riches story. Orphaned at a young age, Esther is taken in by her cousin Mordecai who raises her. Mordecai raised Esther in the Jewish faith and they were proud of their heritage and the promises that were theirs to be claimed.

Ironically, although her story is a story of great faith, there is not one mention of God in the entire book of Esther. Had I not mentioned that to you, you probably wouldn't have noticed it, because when you read the book of Esther you can see God's fingerprints all over it. Yet, there is no mention of Him by name.

At a recent speaking engagement, I was challenged by a woman who had not read the Book of Esther yet questioned why it would be among the books of the Bible if God's name was not mentioned.

Great question and one that is quickly answered if you read the Book of Esther. You see, the name of God is *on* the Book of Esther, even though it is not *in* the book of Esther.

This "omission" teaches us a valuable lesson and one that is depicted beautifully through Esther's story: ***even when God is silent – He is still present.*** God's silence does not mean that He is absent. He is always with us. He is Emmanuel, "God with us."

Has there ever been a time when you have thought God had abandoned you? When you thought that God was absent only to realize that He was with you the entire time? When or how did God make Himself known to you?

God speaks to us through His holy Word. Sometimes, we are fortunate enough to literally hear the voice of God; other times God speaks to us through the events and people surrounding our circumstances.

I have personally dug into the study of discerning God's voice. We want to make sure that we are hearing His still, small voice within us. I have certainly learned that my best ideas are sometimes, well, not so great! I want to be sure that I am hearing from God and the first step in doing so is to *listen.*

Often when we present ourselves before God in prayer and meditate on His Word, we are busy filling the space. Yes, God wants us to have a conversation with Him, but we need to let some margin in place so we can *listen* too. This can be difficult, but it is oh, so necessary! Our lives are filled with busyness and clutter. We need to silence our minds to make space for Him to speak. So, my friend, this may sound harsh, but if you aren't hearing from God perhaps it is simply because you are not listening!

Whether He is speaking to us directly or through someone else, God is with us. Always. Ever present. It all comes back to that question we must reconcile in our heart, "Do we trust God?" Esther certainly did.

This is one of the most beautiful lessons from her story. God, even when silent, is present.

Join me now, and pick up this precious book of the Bible and read her story...

22

Her Story

Christian author and speaker Beth Moore has written a very comprehensive Bible Study series on the Book of Esther. It is a historical as well as spiritual lesson and this amazing study is aptly titled, *"It's Tough Being a Woman!"* Beth reminds us that although we expect God to work through miracles, it is also good to know that God works through the ordinary things not just through the miracles and wonders that we hope for in life. God sets forth a plan for every woman, man, and child that puts their hope in Him. Each of us with a flicker of faith and a thimble of trust are given the same opportunity to live out our destiny in Jesus Christ.[7]

In the Book of Esther, we see the rise of a very common woman. A woman who is thrust into a position of influence by circumstances beyond her control. This ordinary woman, under God's grace does the absolutely extraordinary. Let's see what happens.

First, the characters:

- Haman – highest noble and official of the King; an Agagite (name "Agag" means powerful; angry)

- Mordecai – Jewish cousin of Esther; raised her as his own
- King Xerxes – King of Persia who removes the Queen from her throne during 7 day Festival at the palace for her disobedience in not coming to him when he beckoned for her
- Esther – common girl named Queen; soon to be Queen to all Jews
- Hegai – charge of King's harem; Head Professor of the Persian "Charm School"

Next, the plot:

Queen Vashti is banished because she doesn't give in to the King's commands. Perhaps she is tired of being "Queen on Parade" but at any rate, she doesn't appear in the court when ordered. King Xerxes banishes her for this in his effort to make a point. This was the best he could come up with after meeting with his advisors, all men I might add, who are concerned that the Queen's conduct will "become known to all women, and so they will despise their husbands." (Esther 1:17) A law is written allowing another woman to rise to this royal position.

All the region's virgin girls were brought to the Palace to go under Hegai's charge, including Esther. Esther quickly earns the favor of both Hegai and the King. No one in the King's palace knows that Esther is Jewish.

Mordecai, concerned for his cousin's well-being remains at the Palace gate where he feels close enough to Esther to learn of the daily happenings and offer protection to her. From this vantage point, he learns of a plot to assassinate the King (Esther 2:21-23). Mordecai warns Esther who warns the King.

Haman plots to destroy the Jews when Mordecai refuses to bow down to him at the Palace gate. Haman approaches the King and sneakily receives permission to decree that on a specific date and time, the Jews will be destroyed (Esther 3:8-15).

Mordecai seeks Esther's help in thwarting this plot against their people. In this moment, Esther is about to step into her destiny.

Destiny is a funny thing. In her study, Beth Moore says, "Destiny appoints one, but affects many."[8] We all have a divine appointment on this earth; a destiny. Eve's destiny was to be the mother of sin and the mother of man. Sarah's destiny was to conceive a child in her old age thus bearing witness to the miraculous powers of God and foreshadowing the virgin birth of our Savior. Leah and Rachel's destiny was to be the mothers to the Twelve Tribes of Israel. Ruth's destiny was to be a convert and great-grandmother to David.

Esther's destiny? To be the catalyst in the preservation of God's people.

Wow! Do you think if Esther realized what she was being called to do, she would have gone willingly? Isn't God gracious and good to us to not reveal the future to us all at once? Walking one day at a time into our future allows us to go gently into our calling without all the anxiety and fear that could pile up if we had all of the facts of our assignment up front.

Personally, I praise God for giving it to us in pieces, a bite at a time. If Esther knew what was going to be asked of her in that palace, she may have never gone and her people could have been wiped off the face of the earth.

- What has God called you to do that has been a surprise to you?
- Was there ever a time that you were asked to take on a project or assignment that led to bigger things than you could have ever dreamed of?

We all have been asked to step up in faith. For most of us, the fate of our people is not at stake, but our family might be. Or our church. There are times when we need to speak up and speak out for the safety and security of others. There are times, when in faith, God calls us to speak out against injustice. Then there are times, when God calls us to a life that we never even dreamed of.

There are some key moments in Esther's story that require our meditation. When Mordecai first implores Esther to speak to the King on behalf of the Jewish people, Esther refuses. "It isn't how it works inside the palace," she basically tells him. In chapter 4:12-14, Mordecai's words ring out with such anointing that Esther must ponder the reality of what he is asking her to do.

"Do not think that because you are in the king's house you alone of all the Jews will escape. For if you remain silent at this time, relief and deliverance

for the Jews will arise from another place, but you and your father's family will perish. And who knows but that you have come to your royal position for such a time as this?"

Such a time as this? Are we not **each anointed for such a time as this?**

The next part is amazing. Simply amazing. Esther, in faith, seeks Mordecai's support through fasting and praying.

"Go, gather together all the Jews who are in Susa, and fast for me. Do not eat or drink for three days, night or day. I and my attendants will fast as you do. When this is done, I will go to the king, even though it is against the law. And if I perish, I perish." So Mordecai went away and carried out all of Esther's instructions.

Fasting, praying, obedience. WOW! Now there is a formula for success! Fasting, praying, obedience.

Esther knew the power of fasting, praying and obedience. Fasting is an incredible way to gain heaven's attention and let God know that you are serious about what you are praying for. Jesus showed us the example of fasting. In Matthew 6:16-18, He says, *"...**when you fast,"** not **if** you fast. He goes on to describe fasting as a private matter between you and your Father in heaven.

Many people confuse abstaining with fasting. **Abstaining** is resisting the urge for something; refraining from something. You may abstain from meat on Fridays in Lent, or abstain from chocolate or sweets as a way to live a healthier life.

Fasting is refraining from all kinds of food and drink for religious sacrifice. It is a way to reach heaven and say, "I am serious about this intention that I place before you. So much so, that I will give up food and water and trust that You alone will sustain me for this period of time." Some fasting can incorporate water and even light foods (protein shake, vegetables and fruit). In deciding if a fast is necessary, like Esther, we must pause and pray and see if we are called to fast. Fasting is personal. Fasting, most simply, is another form of prayer.

Go Deeper...

Let's pause here for a moment. What exactly might fasting and praying mean to you?

Incorporating fasting with prayer

Have you ever fasted with prayer for a special intention? Did you fast alone? Did you call upon others to join you? What was the reason? What was the result?

If you have not tried this, how might you be able to incorporate fasting with prayer? Here are a few things I have done that have accelerated my prayer on a particular intention:

- Fast for a period of days as a reminder that this is a focused time of sincere prayer and coming before the Lord
- Fast during the time someone is undergoing surgery. Sometimes we feel helpless as we wait for the call or text from a friend or loved one. Fasting, again, helps to keep you focused on the prayer and the presence of God.
- Skip lunch and during your lunch break read God's word or get on your knees in prayer.

Reserving your fasting for a special occasion

Do you incorporate fasting in your prayer life, or do you only reserve fast days for those assigned by your faith community (Ash Wednesday and Good Friday come to mind.)

It is certainly biblical to abstain from food on designated days. In the first chapters of Genesis, God has even commanded us to abstain from work and rest on the seventh day. Fasting for special occasions could include:

- Abstaining from work on the Sabbath
- Abstaining from gossip
- Fasting from social media
- Fasting from television and Netflix
- Abstaining from eating out and cooking at home
- Abstaining from sexual relations (1 Corinthians 7:5)

Fasting and abstaining from more than food can certainly enhance your prayer life and help you to more fully experience the presence of God.

If you have never fasted

Jesus, Himself, sets the example for prayer and fasting throughout the New Testament. Are you interested in learning more about how and why to fast? I, first, urge you to read what Jesus has said about the subject. You can begin by reading the following verses in Scripture. The following verses contain the topic of fasting but be sure to read them in the greater context of the entire Scripture passage.

Luke 2:37

Luke 4:2-4

Matthew 6:16-18

Luke 18:1-12

Acts 13:2-4

Acts 14:23

I have seen firsthand the benefit of adding fasting to prayer. Jesus Himself teaches about this. In Matthew 17 the disciples bring a demon-possessed boy to Jesus. They beg for mercy on this child and they tell Jesus that they were not able to drive out the evil spirits. Jesus rebuked the demon and it came out of the boy. The disciples question, *"Why couldn't we drive it out?"* In verses 20-21 Jesus replies, *"Because you have so little faith....Nothing will be impossible for you... but this kind does not go out except by prayer and fasting."*

Sacrifice is the way of the Father. He sent His only Son to be sacrificed for our salvation. When we deny ourselves or sacrifice something we want in prayer or praise to Him, it gets his attention. Fasting tells heaven, "I'm serious about this. So much so, that I will give up _____ that you may hear and answer me." Yes, some things in our life can only be driven out by prayer and fasting.

So try it for a day...or two...or three. Reach out to me if you want to have a deeper discussion about this beautiful form of prayer by email at Michele @MicheleGiletto.com. Fasting as described here is not a medical diet or intended for dieting. As always, if you have any questions or health-related concerns around fasting for your particular body and health, please consult your family doctor first.

23

Rooted and Seeking

Let's imagine for a moment what Esther's life was like *before* the crown. She was orphaned. She was a Jew living in a Gentile world. We don't know if her parents were tragically killed, or if they passed from disease or natural causes. Whatever the tapestry of her life was, we can imagine it was difficult, lonely and filled with great uncertainty. Her Uncle Mordecai was, in a way, her own Kinsman-Redeemer. He was the one who took her in and continued to raise her in the faith.

When I consider Esther's story, I am struck over and over again that this book in the Bible does not contain the name of God. As we said earlier, at first pass God appears absent.

Oh, friend, can you relate? Have there been times in your life when you felt like God was completely absent from you? We know in our mind He is ever-present, yet sometimes when the circumstances mount and we don't *feel* His presence, we grow so weary and worried.

Whenever that uncertainty creeps in, I consider Esther. Esther models for us a woman who, first and foremost, is a woman chasing the Lord. A woman who is seeking Him first and constantly. A woman who is rooted in the discipline of prayer and fasting. Don't you desire to be such a woman?

It appears on the surface Esther never once doubted God, and perhaps she didn't. It's easy for us to put women like Esther up on a pedestal and immediately distance ourselves from relating to them. We see only their strengths and we see only our weaknesses.

There was another woman, a modern-day woman, who like Esther lived with such fierce tenacity of faith. Let me tell you her story.

Gonxha Agnes Bojaxhiu was born in 1910 in Skopje, Macedonia. This ordinary woman from an obscure place would go on to change the lives and hearts of millions.

She became a missionary sister who cared for the dying and diseased on the streets of Calcutta, India. Seeing Jesus in the lowest, filthiest, most ravaged and diseased became her sermon. She inspired the world as the simple nun dressed in a white sari with blue borders. Yes, regardless of your religious affiliation, the world knew about this incredibly unselfish nun called Mother Teresa.

Mother Teresa often talked about how distant she felt from God and how often this feeling surrounded her. Yes, a modern-day saint felt more than an arms-length away from the God of her heart. She would question her ability to move forward in her calling. She would question where the provision would come from to pay the bills and keep the lights on. She wondered if she was doing all she was supposed to be doing. Basically, she lived in spiritual torment every day. And she talked about it.

In her book, *"Come be my light,"* Mother Teresa shares her writings all filled with a longing for the Presence of God. She shares the emptiness and desolation she felt while praying. This season of longing lasted nearly fifty years.

> *"Where is my faith? Even deep down, right in, there is nothing but emptiness and darkness. My God — how painful is this unknown pain. It pains without ceasing. I have no faith. I dare not utter the words and thoughts that crowd in my heart and make me suffer untold agony. So many unanswered questions live within me — I am afraid to uncover them — because of the blasphemy. If there be God, please forgive me"*[9]

"If there be God?"

Whenever I consider this suffering of Mother Teresa's heart, I am reminded of the father who approached Jesus to bring out the evil spirit that had possessed his son.

The father speaks to Jesus in the Gospel of Mark:22-24.

> *"...But if you can do anything, take pity on us and help us.*
>
> *'If you can?' said Jesus. 'Everything is possible for him who believes.'*
>
> *Immediately the boy's father exclaimed, 'I do believe; help me overcome my unbelief!'"*

I am forever grateful for this man who spoke so honestly to Jesus. His example has encouraged me to be honest with Jesus when I, as a believer, am filled with any thoughts of unbelief.

What does unbelief look like?

- Sarah not believing she could have a baby at her age.

- Naomi not believing her family's name would ever be redeemed.

- You and I, every time we surrender some person or situation unto the Lord and then take it back and try to control it.

Mother Teresa served well, even during her season of unbelief. She remained obedient to the call on her life to serve others. She loved deeply, even when the well of her own heart appeared to be dried up.

Just as the name of God is absent from the book of Esther, God, Himself, felt absent from Mother Teresa.

Yet both women believed, even amid their unbelief.

Esther in her appointment to save her people.

Mother Teresa in her appointment to save her people.

In 2016, the Catholic Church declared this modest woman a saint. Imagine, a saint whose life is so well documented on video tape and in pictures. A true saint of the 20th century, just like Esther, just like you and me.

For our purposes, however, let's not look at a saint as defined by a church, but a saint as defined by Scripture.

Jesus uses the word "disciple" to describe the holy. The word is used 268 times in the New Testament – through the Gospels and the Book of Acts. And then it is not.

The epistle writers, particularly Paul, tend to use the word "saint" to describe the holy. Paul begins many of his letters to the "saints in…" Each time he uses the word, he follows with language reminding the body of Christ they are indeed holy, chosen and called to be the Father's own through Jesus Christ.

Sister, you are called to be a saint. You have been invited to answer the call that God has on your life, just as Esther answered the call He had for her and Mother Teresa and many others. One of the reasons God put this study in my hands and yours is to remind us of His intense hopes, dreams and plans for us. He desires us to see the similarities with the women of Scripture, not the differences created over thousands of years. You are a saint! You are holy and stand apart in a world filled with resentment and bitterness. You are a light in the darkness and a beacon of hope for everyone you meet. Some of us may be called to the streets of Calcutta like Mother Teresa, or the palace like Esther, but for most of us, Calcutta and the palace can be found in our day-to-day life.

 Go Deeper…

Consider for a moment, the messy, dirty and dark places of your life. What is your Calcutta? Where can you encounter Jesus in those moments? What does it look like? What does He look like? Write your response on the next page.

I see Jesus in the depressed and weary. I see Jesus in the elderly's crippled fingers and failing memory. I see Jesus in a spouse who has suffered greatly by the diseases of his mind, robbing him of hope and a future. But God...God in a moment can correct and restore it all and for this and for this reason alone, I will continue to hope.

Consider for a moment where the bright victories of your life reside? What is your palace? Where have you been victorious? Where have you seen God's redemptive hand turn the ashes into beauty?

I see God's redemption in the lives of my children. Adopted and called into our earthly family as we are all adopted and called into God's heavenly family.. They experience the love of a family and community that tells them daily, "you matter and are important." God has allowed me to witness their bright light even amidst the suffering brought on by caring for a dad ravaged by depression and dementia. God has called us to each other to love BIG and to walk together toward Him. Knowing their faith grows even as life's circumstances mount provides hope and an assurance of God's promise for a mighty future!

Have you ever experienced a season where God felt far off? Absent? How did you respond? Did you remain obedient to what you believed by faith or did you close the door to Him completely?

If you have ever experienced doubts discussed today, how have you overcome it?

For me, seasons of doubt are overcome by remaining disciplined.

Even when praying is difficult, pray anyway...

Even when the Word of God seems arid and dry, read it anyway...

Even when the relationship seems over, love anyway...

Even when there is no appreciation, give anyway...

This is my advice because this has been my experience. Whatever you need to do, do it anyway. Regardless of feelings. Regardless of other's perception. Remember, Noah built the ark while the sun was shining. Obedience and discipline are the keys. And discipline is the first step to sainthood. Be the saint you are called to be.

The world needs your kind of saint.

24

For Such a Time as This

Courage is contagious. When a brave man takes a stand, the spines of others are often stiffened. Billy Graham

Esther teaches us to pause. Even after she realizes the weight of her calling, she pauses. She implores her people to fast and pray for three days. She has created margin in her life and in theirs to allow God to work. Similar to the margins on a paper that create space to allow us to read, comprehend and organize our thoughts, margin in our lives allows the time and space to hear from God, discern His will for us and prepare to carry it out. Margin is an important aspect of the Christian walk, particularly in an age when we are plugged in and available to anyone in the world 24/7. We need margin. We need to insist on creating time and space in our lives to be plugged in to the heavens as much as we are plugged in on earth.

During this time of margin, Esther considers how she may approach the King with her request. When the King sees her, he invites her forward by motioning his royal scepter. When King Xerxes asks her what she wants, she states softly that she would like the pleasure of his company, with

Haman, at a banquet she has prepared. At this time, you may be thinking, "Good call, Esther! Get him on a full stomach and with a little wine in him like Ruth did with Boaz, and then he will grant you your request!" That plan could possibly work, but that is not what Esther does. At the banquet, when the King asks her what he can grant her, she simply states she would like his company, again, tomorrow night at another banquet and of course, Haman is welcome. By this additional pause, Esther completely disarms her adversary, Haman. She is playing into his pride and ego and Haman is believing he is being included because of his great importance (Esther 5:7-14).

Haman, so full of wine and pride, allows his happiness to go to rage when on his way home that blasted Mordecai, once again, refuses to pay homage to him. That night, we learn in chapter six the King cannot sleep. Perhaps it is the weight of his responsibilities, perhaps it is the unfinished business with Esther, perhaps it is the wine, but he cannot sleep and so he calls for the Book of Annals. As he is reading, he learns of an assassination attempt on his life. By God's perfect timing, Haman is outside the door ready to come in and demand Mordecai's life. The King and Haman have an exchange about the King's business first. *"What should be done for the man that the King delights to honor?"* (Esther 6:6-14) Haman, in his pride, assumes the King is speaking about him. He boasts on the delight and honor that should be bestowed on such a man. The King agrees and sends for Mordecai. Mordecai? Haman must be thinking, "How is that slimy rat being honored and not me?" Oh, our Father who art in heaven has just knocked Haman down a few bars!

All of this is occurring as Esther prepares her banquet for Haman and the King. Esther has been patient and has remained laser-focused in fulfilling her responsibility to assist her people. Realize that ultimately Esther could be walking into her own execution by revealing she is a Jew, yet Esther has gone about her work by upholding both the law of God and the law of man. Esther, by not rushing into a willful charade, has allowed for God's perfect timing to take place regarding this situation. Esther also has some knowledge about her opponent. Many times when we are faced with an adversary who has more power than us and has more influence and is louder than us, we can either shrink away or attempt to meet their bombastic nature with our own. Esther does neither. She stays focused on what she needs to do and patiently waits. Had Esther rushed in when the information was first revealed to her, the exchange in chapter 6, verses 6-14 may have not had the chance to occur. Had Esther rushed in with her request at the first meeting with the King in chapter 5 verse 3, she may not have had the same amount of credibility, for it would not yet have been revealed to the King that Mordecai saved his life. Haman could have dismissed her as merely trying to help her cousin. He could have discredited her intentions. But God, in His perfect timing allows the events of redemption to unfold. Yes, Esther's story is about preserving her people through God's perfect timing, by fasting, prayer and obedience to the laws of God and the laws of man.

Esther could have felt cheated out of the life she dreamed of. She could have felt cheated out of being raised by her parents. She could have felt cheated out of a normal life when she was sent to the palace. She was not a woman who desired riches. She was a woman who desired substance. This is what makes her such an interesting leader. Esther was in a position of great influence and yet she remained true to her roots and true to her upbringing. She was not impressed by her surroundings. Some women may have tried to get more out of their position, not Esther.

Esther was a woman of substance, grace and faith. Her story is a beautiful portrayal of leading with integrity and faith. I know many women like Esther. Women who seek God's will in everything they do. Women who pause to hear from God before making major decisions. Women who sacrifice. Women who accept *where* they are instead of pining away for what they *want*. Women who realize they *are chosen, not cheated*. **Esther was not a woman who desired riches. She was a woman who desired substance.**

Go Deeper....

What modern day women can you think of who have stood up against the persecution of another? Look up the following and share some names of your own on the *Discover Yourself in the Women of the Bible* Facebook page:

       1) Rosa Parks

       2) Mother Teresa

       3) Immaculée Ilibagiza

       4) Other?

25

Women of Faith

Eve, Sarah, Leah, Rachel, Ruth Esther & YOU

We end this study with a reflection on the Women in the Old Testament. As we wrap up, there is one more incredible woman to introduce: YOU! Over these past few weeks, I pray you have seen yourself throughout the pages of Scripture as you have pressed in and studied the lives of these magnificent women.

God has given us His Word so we can learn, be inspired and be changed.

Although the physical Bible has been recorded and completed, until Jesus returns in glory, we are still writing the story. Each of us has our own story of life before *knowing* the Lord and can testify to what our life is like now.

I pray you have been encouraged to spend more time in this relationship – the most important relationship of our lives! God desires you to talk to Him and to spend time with Him. His Presence is glorious and as we have seen, wonderful things happen when we know the Lord.

Go Deeper....

Let's take a look at the beautiful women we have studied and see what is reflected back to us when we hold up a mirror.

EVE

Eve reminds me of myself because…

Like Eve, I need to work on…

SARAH

Sarah reminds me of myself because…

Sarah reminds me that I need to work on…

LEAH and RACHEL

Leah reminds me that…

Rachel reminds me that…

Leah and Rachel's story reminds me that I need to…

RUTH

Ruth's story teaches me…

In Ruth's story, I see myself…

ESTHER

Esther's courage reminds me how I...

Esther teaches me that I...

Which woman's story did you most closely identify with?

What do you think God wants to reveal to you through that story?

Write out a sentence for each Woman's life:

Eve = "Guilty but Forgiven"

Sarah = "Her disbelief turned to wonder"

Leah = "Unloved yet redeemed"

Rachel = "Loved but lost"

Ruth = "Refuses rejection; chooses redemption"

Esther = "Faith and courage in preserving God's people"

Write a prayer of thanksgiving to God for all He has revealed to you in the study of the Old Testament's leading ladies.

Father, we thank You for these courageous women. These women were hand-picked and anointed by You, just as You have hand-picked and anointed the woman reading this. Father, as we walk into our own destiny, let us always remember that we are picked out, not picked on, by You. Help us to always approach Your "throne of grace with confidence, so that we may receive mercy and find the strength to help us in our time of need." (Hebrews 4:16)

We love You, God. We trust You. We believe in You. Thank You for Your unwavering belief in us and for Your abounding love. Thank You, Father, that even when You are silent, You remain ever-present with us. You stun me, Lord, with Your greatness. Amen.

Thank you...

...for taking this journey with me through the Old Testament.

These women are just like us. What a privilege to spend time with them, and you, all in the presence of our most holy Father. May each lesson be a blessing to you now, or be a blessing in the future.

May you remember we are blessed, not broken. We can triumph over temptations. We take our worth from the Word of God, not from the world.

May you remember you have been created for such a time as this. You are not cheated, but chosen to be exactly where you are at this exact moment.

We turn ourselves over to the care of Jesus and by the Spirit commit to spending time in prayer, in worship and in God's Word.

May your life make a difference in the story of the building of the kingdom within the Body of Christ.

May God be praised for every good and gracious deed that you have done and for all the love in your heart for our Lord and Savior, Jesus Christ. To God be all the glory, now and forever! Amen.

About the Author

Michele Giletto is a woman who prays. She is a wife, mom, Bible study teacher and speaker. Her calling is to reach women, in all stages of life, and help them move from routine religion to life-giving faith that only comes from personally knowing Jesus.

Her love of prayer and Scripture led her to begin *Gathered in Grace Prayer Ministry* in 2012. Michele is also co-founder, with Deborah Lovett, of the dynamic online women's faith community called *Women Gathered*.

A full-time healthcare administrator, Michele is a dedicated wife and mother to her two children.

To learn more about Michele and for information on how to engage her for your upcoming event, visit

www.MicheleGiletto.com

Michele @MicheleGiletto.com

END NOTES

[1] National Resource Center & Health from website: www.nrchealth.com.

[2] *New Living Translation, NLT* (Tyndale House Publishers, 2008).

[3] Webster's Dictionary Online at www.merriam-webster.com/dictionary.

[4] Online Resource for Scripture Verses at www.OpenBible.info.

[5] Online Resource quoted from website: www.womenintheancientworld.com.

[6] Rabbinical teaching confirmed through www.Chabad.org.

[7] John Maxwell, *The Maxwell Leadership Bible* (Thomas Nelson, 2014) 20, print.

[8] John Maxwell, *The Maxwell Leadership Bible* (Thomas Nelson, 2014) 20, print.

[9] *New Living Translation Study Bible, NLT* (Tyndale House Publishers, 2008) 60, print.

[10] Beth Moore, *Esther: It's Tough Being a Woman* (LifeWay Press, 2008)

[10] Beth Moore, *Esther: It's Tough Being a Woman* (LifeWay Press, 2008)

[11] Mother Teresa and Brian Kolodiejchuk, *Come be My Light* (Doubleday Religion, an imprint of the Crown Publishing Group, a division of Random House, Inc., New York, 2007)

Made in the USA
Middletown, DE
10 May 2019